WITHDRAWN

AIRBRUSHED NATION

AIRBRUSHED NATION

NATION
THE LURE & LOATHING OF WOMEN'S MAGAZINES

Jennifer Nelson

SEAL PRESS

AIRBRUSHED NATION
The Lure & Loathing of Women's Magazines

Copyright © 2012 Jennifer Nelson

Published by
Seal Press
A Member of the Perseus Books Group
1700 Fourth Street
Berkeley, California 94710

Library of Congress Cataloging-in-Publication Data

Nelson, Jennifer, 1965-
  Airbrushed nation : the lure and loathing of women's magazines / by
Jennifer Nelson.
     p. cm.
  ISBN 978-1-58005-413-3
  1. Women's periodicals, American. 2. Women--Press coverage--United
States. 3. Women's periodicals, American--Illustrations--Themes, motives.
4. Women in mass media. 5. Body image in women--Social aspects--United
States. I. Title.
  PN4879.N47 2012
  051.082--dc23
                            2012012417

9 8 7 6 5 4 3 2 1

Cover design by Erin Seaward-Hiatt
Interior design by Tabitha Lahr
Printed in the United States of America
Distributed by Publishers Group West

For Ashley—and all the beautiful women
reading a magazine everywhere

Contents

Introduction

Often, aspiring magazine writers cut their professional teeth writing for smaller newspapers and magazines before transitioning to the big leagues of national magazines. Not me. I knew what I wanted. I'd grown up with my girly nose buried in the glossy pages of everything from *Tiger Beat* and *Young Miss* to *Cosmo, Shape,* and *Self.* I was enthralled and occasionally appalled, but still I was totally smitten.

At the time, it didn't occur to me that these women's magazines, which had imparted a lifetime's worth of seemingly friendly advice to me on everything from dating and sex to fashion and health, approached its readers as if they needed fixing, nor did I think my self-esteem and self-worth had been diminished simply by reading their shiny pages. In fact, like millions of other women readers, I craved their content and made no connection that any of my insecurities could be traced back to women's magazines.

So when it came time to launch my career, I went straight to the source of the love—the perfumed pages of the chick slicks. One of the very first pitch letters I sent went to *Woman's Day,* one of the nation's oldest and most widely read women's magazines. I had what I believed was a solid story idea about smoking cessation, and a lot of hope. About all I had going for me was my tenacity in sending an article idea to them, along with my crossed fingers; after all, I was green and *WD* had been around so long, it sat on my mother's coffee table when I was a kid. So when the health editor called me three days later, I was ecstatic.

Though my pitch didn't pan out, the editor did assign me another story, and for the next thirteen years I crafted the very articles I used to love to read, for magazines including *Ladies' Home Journal, Self, Fitness, Oprah, Cosmo, Glamour, Redbook,* and the rest. While most of my writing centered around health, fitness, and nutrition—work I was proud of—I'm guilty of having crafted stories that were less transparent, ones written to fit the editor's agenda, not what my reporting had sussed out. Whether it was getting real women or expert sources to say exactly what my editor wanted them to say in a quote, or being selective about the women who were profiled in "real women" stories, I've jumped through my share of editorial hoops. I've also written my share of the "drop five, ten, or fifteen pounds" articles that plaster those perfumed pages. In other words, I'm guilty of giving you, women readers, the same type of magazine content I take to task in the following pages as being misleading, undermining, fear-mongering, or fluffy.

However, between the dredge and the dreck, and the airbrushed ideal, value can still be found between the glossy covers: whether it's informative health stories or an exposé on social issues, solid advice on parenting, or helpful information on fitness, I have had the privilege of writing good stuff that doesn't demean, hype, or undermine. I've worked with smart editors with integrity—both male and female—who valued transparency in the women's glossies.

Unfortunately, this is the exception to the rule. The more deeply entrenched I became in the perfumed pages of the chick slicks, the more deeply troubled I was by the loss of women's magazines the way *I* remembered them: as a girl's best friend, a funk-lifting pick-me-up, an inspirational forum for advice on how to look and feel your best, get the job you want, and have better sex—with a few celebrity interviews and fashion spreads thrown in for fluffy measure. With each decade, it seemed, the once fairly innocuous content found in women's glossies had gotten increasingly more destructive, dumbed down, and airbrushed to surreal perfection. When I became more conscious that these magazines were continually trying to make readers over, often implying that women needed to constantly improve themselves—either directly or through inference—I began to scrutinize them more critically.

Suddenly, I wanted every woman to take a closer look at what they were actually reading, especially now that I had a daughter who was reading these very glossies herself. Now each image that my daughter and her peers viewed had me wondering if the image was airbrushed or retouched, and if the dieting and weight loss, dating and sex advice, and information on health, well-being, and beauty should be challenged rather than accepted at face value.

Was some of the content derogatory, demeaning, or sexist, and if so, was my daughter buying into it? Was the airbrushed imagery affecting the self-worth of young women her age, or hell, even women *my* age? Was being a regular reader of the chick slicks a tutorial on an airbrushed ideal that drove women to self-destructive behaviors like eating disorders, needless cosmetic surgery, and an obsession with appearance over substance? I wanted to know the truth. And I wanted other women to know it, too.

So why *do* we buy these magazines, if they're so destructive? Because despite the things we might loathe about them, we're drawn even more by what they promise to provide: an escapist read in between loads of laundry or during our coffee break, poolside on a chaise lounge, or waiting for a doctor's appointment. There is no work required here. It's all about the desire to be entertained, inspired, moved, maybe snag a new chicken recipe or hairstyling tip, or indulge our fascination with celebrity lifestyles. Bottom line is that we'd like to believe these scented pages were put together specifically with our interests, lifestyles, and well-being in mind.

But the further we get into the pages of these magazines, the experience often feels less like an easy escape and more like a passport to slow-creeping angst. The too-thin models taunt our self-esteem with their impossible perfection, the fashion spreads of expensive clothes and accessories depress us with their ridiculous price tags, the articles insult our intelligence with their patronizing tone, the "real women" who are surveyed, interviewed, or quoted smack of phoniness, while still other editorial content unsettles us with its fear-mongering.

Let's get real, ladies, because the magazines certainly aren't! Not only do they make promises they can't keep; they also create false expectations about what our lives should look like. It's an airbrushed ideal, one where readers are left wondering, "Wow, can I really save my marriage with this simple move in bed? Can I truly turn back the hands of time by ten years in one week?" Um, the reality is no.

Of course, this doesn't make the chick slicks evil or the only media to blame. TV, advertisers, the Internet, movies—all media play a role. But while we can't change the way members of the media think or portray reality, we can change the way *we* think. We can learn to use our critical minds to distinguish what's real from what's false within the pages, and we can choose to support more realistic ideals. We can choose to denounce the images or content that makes us feel that we don't measure up. We can shun subject matter that makes us feel inadequate. Knowing you're being force-fed an unreal paradigm makes it easier to withdraw yourself from that which strips your sense of self.

●   ●   ●

I still love the women's glossies for what is good within them, and for all they strive to be on a good month. There is still great writing on their silken pages, awesome writers still in the trenches, incredibly talented editors toiling away—some stoically and others disheartened. And there are still women bold and brazen enough to put their truth on the page for us to read and benefit from. That's what I still love and admire about the glossies.

Whether you love women's glossies or loathe them, or fall somewhere in between, I hope you will be both enlightened and perhaps occasionally surprised by what you learn in the following pages, but in particular, I hope it provides some insight into the impact women's magazines have on us as women.

Chapter 1

A CHICK-SLICK HISTORY

Magazines will never die because there is a visceral feeling
of having that thing in your hands and turning the pages.
It's so different on the screen. It's the difference between
looking at a woman and having sex with her.
—George Lois, former *Esquire* art director

From their earliest incarnations, women's magazines have held our interest, and they continue to do so today. While competing media and changes in society may have altered the content of women's magazines over time, in some ways it's as relevant and unchanged today as it was more than two centuries ago, when the first women's book was published. Today's chick slicks still work from the premise that readers want and need to improve themselves. And why wouldn't they? We've been conditioned from the very first magazine to glean advice, inspiration, and entertainment from our glossy copies, and editors continue to diligently work to please their audience—a community of women. The roots of the women's magazines that grace your coffee table today are firmly planted in the pages of the magazines of the past.

1

(WAY) BACK IN THE DAY

In 1792, about fifty years after the first general interest magazine hit the stands, a publication strictly designed for women appeared named *The Lady's Magazine and Repository of Entertaining Knowledge*. Though short-lived, this mouthful of a magazine was the first for American women. It was the first time in history that women were thought to need a magazine—a paper room of their own. The magazine was written deliberately for women, about women, and because of women. A three-hundred-page volume came out every six months, filled with poetry, prose, literature reviews, even foreign news, and it was designed to inspire the female mind.

The glossy seed was sown, and women's magazines began to sprout on to the early American scene. One successful example was *Godey's Ladies Book* (1830–1898). When Louis A. Godey began *Godey's Ladies Book,* the magazines were distributed via mail throughout the country. Early magazines like *Godey's* relied on subscriptions for their revenue, and while other magazines unleashed during this era lasted only two to four years, *Godey's*—which came out monthly—survived over three decades.[1]

Godey's included a variety of content, mostly short stories and poetry. Both readers and Editor-in-Chief Sarah Hale, who was one of the first and few female editors at the time, provided much of the magazine's content. Hale invited her readers to send in their poems, essays, and stories, and they responded in droves. Magazine articles were occasionally penned by popular writers of the time, such as Edgar Allen Poe, but the majority of the magazine's fiction arrived via unpaid contributors—mainly women readers. (Interesting that *Ladies' Home Journal* launched a similar plan in 2012 known as "crowd sourcing," in which a large volume of their content is to be contributed by readers with fresh voices.) Though

Hale was one early editor-in-chief of a women's magazine, these burgeoning glossies were helmed mostly by men, who presumed to understand and deliver what women reader's desired.

Why the long gap between *The Lady's Magazine* and the successful launch of *Godey's*? Aside from the fact that women were considered second-class citizens at the time, there were also circulation issues. The only way to move magazines effectively was through the mail. Yet until the Postal Act of 1784, individual postmasters around the country were authorized to choose and distribute only the magazines *they* saw fit. Unfortunately, women's magazines, often called "books," were not deemed important enough to warrant the distribution effort.[2]

And what did these women's magazines pack inside? To start, the pubs were padded with lots of "interesting facts," otherwise known as "filler" (much the same way magazines are today), with short pieces that included studies and statistics (a diddy on how to be a proper lady, or the appropriate airing of beds, or the growth of women's education). Other goodies included sheet music, travel stories, essays, and colorful, hand-painted fashion "plates," which were thick cardboard inserts that illustrated the current fashions. *Godey's* also covered "personal topics," usually in the form of Dear Abby-like columns, which likely inspired readers to identify intimately with the magazine, since it offered advice on love, relationships, and social dilemmas of the time (including dealing with gossip or misbehaving servants, the proper age to marry, and reminders that passion was a requisite for a happy marriage and not just esteem).[3]

But with the invasion of England's Education Act and a booming trade industry, society began to shift and so did the magazines. Women suddenly had more job options, so domestic servants were harder to hire. Families who employed household help now found themselves without extra hands.

As women began to manage more of their own domestic duties, the magazines covered them in full force. Many began introducing handy household hints, advice, even detailed recipes. More than a century later, these topics still remain staples in today's women's glossies.

These women's magazines not only targeted women readers, but they also provided an outlet for women writers and editors to demonstrate their talents, an opportunity not yet extended to them by general interest magazine publishers. The earliest magazines wrote to an elite class of women readers—generally middle- and upper-class wives and daughters, suffragists, and educated women. They were yet to include advertising but were chock-full of literature, fashion plates, and etiquette advice.

As a result, the women's magazines that popped up in the decades before the Civil War look startlingly similar to glossies we see on the stands today. Readers relied on and trusted the information printed in the pages, giving the editors incredible power and responsibility.

It wasn't until *Delineator* (1863–1937) came out that women actually got a taste of a true fashion rag. While *Godey's* contained fashion plates, they were simply color illustrations rather than fashion advice. *Godey's* advised women on how to dress from an

GLOSSY FACT

America's first true fashion rag was *Harper's Bazaar,* published in 1867. Nearly 150 years later, it's still running strong, with more than half a million readers. Today, it bills itself as the most "sophisticated, elegant, and provocative" fashion resource for women.

ethical standpoint rather than from a style perspective. In *Delineator,* publisher Ebenezer Butterick nixed articles about women appearing clean and chaste, and the health dangers of wearing corsets and hoops, and after having invented tissue paper dress patterns, he included one in every issue, which created a bulky but downright desirable magazine.[4]

GLOSSY FACT

Vogue launched in 1892 and started as a weekly magazine for high-society New Yorkers. Early covers featured coiffed young women known as "Gibson Girls," named after the illustrator who created the look. In the 1960s, the magazine concentrated on fashion, making models household names, and contained openly sexual article content.

At the time, only wealthy women could afford expensive fashions. Affluent American women, for example, had casts made of their bodies and sent them to dressmakers abroad, who shipped back miniature versions of their designs for approval—worn on dolls, no less. You can only imagine the expense and time involved in this convoluted process. With *Delineator,* suddenly just about any woman could afford to make her own fashions, thanks to a free pattern in her favorite magazine.

McCall's and *Vogue* jumped on this fashion bandwagon. In addition to articles and short stories, they included clothing advice as well. This was how fashion magazines took root, becoming catalogs for the clothes and accessories available in the stores (see more on fashion in chapter 4). Being in style became a feminine prerogative, and women's magazines became the standard resource for American women to learn about fashion crazes and foibles. A new era of fashion magazine publishing had begun.

THE BIG SIX AND BEYOND

By the end of the nineteenth century, six leading women's magazines surpassed all others in sales. And by the beginning of the twentieth century, these magazines attracted advertising revenue and a loyal readership of women. The "Big Six," as they became known, were *Delineator, McCall's, Ladies' Home Journal, Woman's Home Companion, Good Housekeeping,* and *Pictorial Review.*[5] They all included articles, short stories, and reader correspondence, as well as fashion, fiction, and poetry. These early lady magazines also provided advice on cleaning, cooking, childcare, and fulfilling the needs of a husband—hence, the start of the how-to-please-your-man focus that would pervade so much of the content in twentieth and twenty-first century chick slicks (more on this in chapter 9, The Big O).

With their low subscription rates, these journals soon reached hundreds of thousands of female readers across the nation, becoming the preferred method for advertisers to market and sell products and services to women, and a popular method women embraced. With income to ride on and a burgeoning readership, magazines began expanding their content.

Profiles of well-known personalities also became staples and reader favorites. They ranged from popular actresses and royalty to successful society women. For instance, you might read about Harriet Quimby, the first woman to master an airplane, or about clothing designer Madame Paquin and her latest fashions. Celebrities, operatic singers, and actresses eventually became a big draw, and women readers ate those stories up—much like they do today. Fiction was also a staple by the early twentieth century, most often written by popular male writers, including Henry Wadsworth Longfellow and Nathaniel Hawthorne. As were nonfiction articles on political, cultural, and social topics relevant to the times. Magazines also included plenty of prescriptive content. Everything—from tainted food and drugs or contaminated drinking water to dirty stores and venereal disease—was covered in the pages of these publications, often in an alarmist way, making them the precursors to the fear-factor articles we read in today's women's magazines (more on this in chapter 7). The stories played on a woman's desire to protect her family and stay knowledgeable about controversial current issues.

But it wasn't all fluff, fiction, and fear-mongering. In the early twenties, women's journals focused on important social issues, such as the suffragist movement. Articles on child psychology and interior decorating also appeared as typical fodder around the 1920s, helping women manage both their home and their child's psyche.

In these early years, the predominantly male editors of women's magazines—including all of the Big Six—put their stamp

GLOSSY FACT

Founded in 1903, *Redbook* derived its name from its first editor, Trumbull White, because he claimed that "red is the color of happiness."[6] Today, the publication has a circulation of just over two million readers.

of individuality on each publication, sometimes in progressive, prowomen ways. One editor of *Pictorial Review* was said to have turned his magazine from "thin and lacking clear direction" to one that published popular fiction and a number of controversial topics, such as birth control and sex education, fostering reader devotion.[7]

An editor of *Delineator,* when asked to make the magazine "softer," reportedly told staffers to send a letter to readers and ask if they want a "namby-pamby magazine."[8]

Yet these two editors may have been the exceptions.

When asked what type of reader *Woman's Home Companion* targeted, the male editor-in-chief at the time said she was "about the same type of woman as the average member of a small-town Congregational or Presbyterian Church."[9]

Naturally, the few magazines that bantered about sex tried to lead the pack by running forbidden or controversial topics. However, they were limited to the sexual facts of life and education about venereal disease. After one sex article in *Ladies' Home Journal,* the magazine reportedly received hundreds of angry letters from readers cancelling their subscriptions. *Pictorial Review* published a list of birth control pros and cons, advocating that the only pro was better health for women by not constantly reproducing.[10]

But this brief efflorescence into more daring, even profeminist, content was largely derailed by the unstable times and the downfall of the economy.

REGROUPING DURING THE DEPRESSION

After the giddy first decades of the twentieth century, one in which women enjoyed greater freedom of expression (think the culture of the flappers, for one), the Great Depression hit with a vengeance, ending this zeitgeist. Sadly, the economic downslide during the thirties put a halt to frivolous topics. Women's journals continued to include social and political content, but began to focus much more on women as homemakers and sex objects, subjects that often became intrinsically linked.

Magazine advertisements began to appear that showed sultry beauties and provocatively dressed women juxtaposed in domestic settings pitching some kitchen or home product, and magazines used similarly styled images in articles about keeping a tidy house or pleasing a man through cooking. Women dressed in heels and pearls were shown scrubbing a floor or baking a pie, foreshadowing that once they finished their menial housework, they were still desirable, sexy creatures for a man's pleasure.

GLOSSY FACT

Woman's Day, which was first published in 1931 as a free in-store recipe planner at A&P supermarkets, today boasts a readership of twenty million. The average reader is in her midthirties, 56 percent of whom are married. *WD* boasts over three million in subscriptions, and readers can still snag a copy at the checkout counter for $2.59.

To fight the forces of the economic tide, including plummeting ad revenues, magazines began appearing in stores as point-of-sale items rather than through the mail via subscription. This shaved overhead costs significantly—from marketing to a subscriber base and maintaining it, to eliminating the expense of shipping to readers. *Family Circle,* which launched in 1932, became the second successful in-store distributed magazine. The publisher sold it to chain grocers like Piggly Wiggly and Sanitary Grocery Co. (later renamed Safeway), and the stores gave magazines away to customers free of charge.[11] Dozens of similar magazines were given away in grocers during the 1930s. *Family Circle,* like *Woman's Day,* was distributed only in stores, and both succeeded. Women shopping for food would presumably scoop them up while waiting at the checkout counter. A savvy selling ploy, to be sure, and one that's still a significant part of the magazine sales system we see today.

GLOSSY FACT

The Seven Sisters were the seven women's magazines traditionally targeted to married homemakers. The name came from the Greek myth of the "seven sisters," or the seven daughters of the titan Atlas. In the myth, Zeus immortalized the sisters in the sky by creating the constellation Pleiades. The magazines were so named because they were at one time a constellation of the most well-known seven women's magazines, dubbed "sister publications," and their editors had largely arrived from the Seven Sister colleges (a cluster of liberal Northeast U.S. colleges that were at one time limited to women).[12]

Perhaps because *Family Circle* and *Woman's Day* continued for many years as magazines found solely at the grocer's, the twin publications found their niche outlasting every other grocery rag. Today both belong to the group of women's magazines that became known as the "Seven Sisters" (see sidebar on p. 10), which

GLOSSY FACT

In 1939, *Good Housekeeping* rocked the woman's magazine industry with a scandal related to its Seal of Approval, a program used by *GH* to lure readers to their magazine by rating consumer products. The Federal Trade Commission (FTC) filed a complaint against *GH,* charging it with "deception in its acts and practices relating to how it issued guarantees of its seal, citing false and exaggerated claims."[13] The case lasted two years and rival magazine staffers at *Ladies' Home Journal* and *McCall's* testified against their sister publication in hopes that the Seal of Approval would be considered unfair competition. (Yet it was an idea *GH* thought up first!) In the end, Hearst received a limp slap on the wrist and was ordered to merely alter the wording of its guarantee. Despite the scandal, readers remained loyal to *Good Housekeeping* whose Seal of Approval is still an iconic and trusted testament of quality today.

included *Ladies' Home Journal, McCall's, Good Housekeeping, Better Homes and Gardens,* and *Redbook*—though you may as well dub these grocery-only twins the two stepsisters, since they were, and still are, largely similar to one another.

SHIFTING TIMES, SHIFTING CONTENT

Despite these changing economic times, women continued to read magazines—if for nothing else than escapism and entertainment. Magazines now provided women with a connection to the larger world outside their own and educated them on the latest products, money-saving tips, and fashion trends. Advice and features on housekeeping and childcare continued to draw women in, and attracting and keeping a man persisted as a theme in women's books across the board.

One *Vogue* editor of the time commented that "pleasing the reader" made the best magazine, but she patronizingly had to include content that was for the "best interest" of the reader.[14] This, of course, assumed she knew what that was. Editors were not above manipulating readers, either. Herbert Mayes, an editor-in-chief of *Good Housekeeping,* admitted he fashioned a phony name to the masthead so he could fabricate a phony editorial firing if a controversy erupted over content.[15] If readers deluged the magazine with complaint letters, he could satisfy reader indignance by simply removing a name from the masthead, as if he'd fired the underling in charge of the story.

Eventually, editors began to assign stories rather than just wait to see what came in from contributors. Loring Schuler, an editor-in-chief of *Ladies' Home Journal,* confessed to calculating a formula with which he developed content for his publication: 38 percent happiness, 37 percent entertainment, 25 percent general information.[16] Each editor had their own preference, likes, and dislikes, which influenced content.

Many of the other magazines no doubt formed similar percentages of formulaic content, which today has evolved into the fixed departments, sections, and recurring columns we're familiar with in the glossies. Editors then could acquire content to fit recurring themes—say, the feel-good essay, the investigative story, the childcare-related piece, and the how-to-land-a-man article.

As the economy tilted back toward equilibrium, magazine sales increased and advertisers began to expand their budgets. This new income allowed editors to lure top writers to their journals, but they did so with difficulty, since these magazines were still considered vehicles primarily for fluffy or "fairy" stories. Though some writers were indeed women, a large majority of contributors were males, who were then tasked with crafting stories and content of interest to the female reader, something often quite foreign to them. Worse, many male writers felt that writing for the women's books was beneath them, despite the pay being some of the best in the magazine world. Writing for the "less intelligent" sex wasn't considered as appealing as writing for traditional men's or general interest magazines.[17] They believed the assignments, which covered topics such as the joy of household tasks, gardening, and cooking, were "fluff." Unfortunately, they were at the mercy of the editors and publishers, who believed these were the topics that women wanted to read about. Sadly, but not totally without merit, those prejudices continued among not only writers and readers but also with the public at large, and fluff became a descriptive catchphrase still used today to describe women's glossies.

Not only did some writers consider the content in these magazines dreck, but when their more important pieces on politics or issues of the day were accepted for publication, they also resented that their material was surrounded by gardening advice and love-lorn tribulations.

Despite the reservations of many of the writers of the day, during both world wars, women's books played a noteworthy role in preaching conservation and how women could help in the war effort. In fact, during World War II, women's mags encouraged the campaign for American women to work outside the home and fill the jobs that men were forced to abandon when they went off to war.[18]

By the 1950s, with the war over and women put back in their place—the home—magazines again shone the spotlight on domestic chores.

THE ERA OF NICHE MAGAZINES

The 1950s also marked another shift for the magazine industry, which faced increased competition from new media, primarily television. It was during this era that TV viewing became much more widespread. Televisions were the must-have appliance in homes, and families scheduled their evenings around favorite shows. Naturally, television drew away both readers and advertisers from the glossies, which had long dominated the limited media world at the time. In response to being bested in the entertainment niche—after all, how could a static, one-dimensional article compete with a moving, talking story in a box—magazines focused more on concrete information and how-to content. Advice articles, such as "How to Manage your Household Chores" and "6 Steps to Make the Dinner Hour More Relaxing for Your Husband," became staples that readers could clip, save, and return to over and over—another tactic we see in women's magazines today.

The media squeeze-out, coupled with the culture's aggressive agenda to firmly reestablish women's subservience to men, increased the magazine industry's hyperfocus on the homemaker. Out of this grew the apron-clad ideal of the perky, pretty fifties housewife, who appeared suddenly like a Stepford Wife in product ads, articles, and as iconic characters in television shows. But this idealized version of the American housewife chafed at women early on, primarily because it didn't reflect real life. The age of the airbrushed ideal was taking root. One housewife, who received a *Ladies' Home Journal* makeover in the early fifties, complained that the magazine presented an ideal impossible for women to live up to. She claimed the magazines flaunted the false notion that women should be on pedestals and also be skilled housewives, seamstresses, decorators, cooks, mothers, and lovers, ensuring they could land and keep their man.

The woman, Julia Ashenhurst, a housewife, wrote:

> *I cannot but question the wisdom and fairness of presenting me as the wife of a teacher and mother of four young children in clothes not my own with a face and hairdo not my own. Even my waist was not my own, for I was hooked into a cinch corset which was nearly the end of me. How will my counterpart in apartments, farms, and developments all over the country feel as she sees this glamorous clotheshorse and realizes that she cannot afford to dress like that and wonders why she cannot look like that?*[19]

That was 1951.

By the late fifties, fiction in the magazines began to decline with the increase in popular television shows and cheap paperback book prices. To win back advertisers, women's titles divided the magazine market into demographics that shared similar characteristics and interests. There was no dearth of niche "audiences": working moms, women over fifty, African American women, middle-class housewives interested in interior design, etc. Breaking readers into these targeted groups was good news for advertisers, and the entire magazine industry went this route. This set the standard for the magazines we see today, and it resulted in an explosion of new publications to target those special interest groups, who in turn attracted their own brand of advertisers: home and decorating magazines attracted appliance ads and paint companies, fitness and health magazines drew in vitamin distributors and athletic clothing labels. Fashion magazines lured shoe, bag, and clothing designers—along with beauty product manufacturers and perfume companies. It was niche marketing at its finest, and everyone wanted a piece of the glossy pie.

GLOSSY FACT

In 1952, *Good Housekeeping* started an anti-cigarette campaign—twelve years before the surgeon general's warning was even printed on cigarette packs—by refusing to accept tobacco advertisements. While research was just starting to link cigarettes and lung cancer, *GH* thought that advertising a potential harmful product would not bode well for their consumer-safety focus.[20]

As a result, by the 1960s, many chick slicks were commercial successes. One top seller was *Cosmopolitan,* today one of the best-selling and most controversial lady magazines out there, due to its sex-centric focus. *Cosmo,* as it's often referred to, was initially published as a fiction magazine in the early twentieth century, then revamped in 1965 to address the needs and desires of single women. The editor, Helen Gurley Brown, and the magazine's advertisers, recognized the needs of single women with disposable income and a desire for a magazine where issues like sex, sexual prowess, birth control, and the power of so-called "feminine wiles" were covered—even exploited—to their best effect.

GLOSSY FACT

Glamour, which launched in 1939 and focused on fashion, beauty, and relationships for the modern young woman, was the first women's magazine to put a black woman on its cover in 1968.

Other niche magazines of the time included *The Advocate,* launched in 1967, which paved the way for other gay and lesbian magazines; and *Essence,* the first major consumer publication aimed at African American women, which opened advertiser's eyes to black women's buying power in 1970. Other mags began to target readers by ethnicity, like *Latina* and *Moderna.* When *Ms.* magazine, which popularized the feminist movement, hit stands in 1972, it shattered the mold by publishing articles about women's rights, politics, sexuality, and violence against women, which, during that time, was an elephant in the room that was rarely, if ever, mentioned in mainstream women's magazines.

GLOSSY FACT

Lear's, a magazine that targeted the over-forty woman, opened the door to marketing to older women but it didn't survive. It would take twenty more years before the industry saw another attempt at reaching the more mature woman, with the successful launch of *MORE* magazine in 1998.

Another magazine that targeted the liberated reader was *Working Woman,* which launched in 1976 and was the first magazine to focus exclusively on workplace, financial, and career advice for women. Not surprisingly, by the early seventies, the standard doctrine of women's magazines began to clash with feminism and its ideals. In 1970, feminists held a sit-in at *Ladies' Home Journal.* The editor-in-chief at the time, John Mack Carter, promised change. He even tried to crush the confrontation by publishing a special eight-page supplement titled "The New Feminism," which appeared in the magazine. However, not much changed. A year later, Carter was quoted as saying, "Some of the complaints made about our magazine by the women's lib types were right. There had been a lot of silliness cranked out to sell products and lifestyles to women, but it will never happen in this magazine again."[21]

Carter went on to edit *Good Housekeeping* in 1975, though how much influence the protests had on the vision he brought to the pages of that journal is debatable.

Ultimately, the volcanic social changes of the sixties and seventies provided the launching point for various publications, while other magazines did what they could to keep up with the times, often reinventing themselves to stay solvent in an increasingly competitive market. Some succeeded; some didn't.

GLOSSY FACT

Self magazine, one of the first women's publications to focus exclusively on nutrition, health, fitness, and beauty, was launched in 1978. Today, *Self* enjoys a 2.7 million monthly audience and focuses on inspiring women's fitness, diet, health, and happiness.

CHANGE AMONG THE SEVEN SISTERS

During the second half of the century, the two stepsisters among the seven—*Woman's Day* and *Family Circle*—continued to flourish. But as it goes among siblings, competition was fierce between the two. To differentiate itself from *Woman's Day, Family Circle* took an interesting editorial turn in the 1980s by running juicy investigative features on issues of interest to women, including toxic waste and hazardous chemicals, cluster diseases, and other fear-factor topics that women wanted to learn about to protect themselves and their families. *Family Circle* became a leader in investigative magazine journalism, but other magazines joined the pursuit, including another lifer: *Redbook*.

After peddling itself as a general interest fiction magazine in the early twentieth century, *Redbook* was recast as another one of the Seven Sisters. In the forties, it focused on young married women, adding more nonfiction. Its circulation climbed. In the 1970s, the magazine targeted moms. During these years, *Redbook* was thought of as the most intellectual of the sisters and today boasts a readership that exceeds two million.[22] With its sale to the Hearst Corporation in the 1980s, it was again rebranded to appeal to women in the twenty-five to forty-four age bracket, with articles on career, home, and family. More fashion and beauty were added, and provocative pieces like "Is There Sex after Motherhood?" and "Why I Date Your Husband" appeared.[23]

In the early 1990s, *Redbook* was labeled the older sister to titles like *Cosmo* and *Glamour*. It was promoted to advertisers as the "juicy *Redbook*."[24] Yet with time, this once supposed hybrid fell in among the sisters as just another one of the seven popular women's glossies.

By the 1970s, the Seven Sisters also included *Better Homes and Gardens,* a former gardening and home magazine that morphed into a chick slick over time.

Originally titled *Fruit, Garden, and Home*, the magazine evolved from the 1950s to target the home do-it-yourselfer with articles on food, decorating, gardening, and family. Advertisers of home appliances, furniture, and garden supplies shepherded the journal, sending its ad revenue soaring and lumping it in with the other six true women's books. All but beauty and fashion were missing from the magazine, but by the eighties, they too had found their way into the magazine's content as publishers tried to please every woman interested in home décor and gardening by adding traditional women's magazine fare like health, beauty, money, and fashion.

But not all the Seven Sisters settled comfortably into their twilight years. *McCall's,* one of the earliest sisters, met an untimely death when television personality Rosie O'Donnell dared to take over the 103-year-old title in 2000 and revamp the book with her vision, and with her at its helm.

Insider Input

"I wanted a magazine that celebrates real women, that understands that they care about more than waistlines or the latest makeup styles or fashions, that they want to be relevant and help each other and care about the world." [25]
—Rosie O'Donnell, talking about taking over *McCall's*

Unfortunately, *Rosie* (the rebranded title) folded two years later. The actress/comedienne/talk-show host reportedly had problems with the publisher, Gruner & Jahr, stating "she could no longer put her face to a publication that didn't reflect her values."[22] Though she was editor-in-chief, the publisher's ideas apparently clashed with Rosie's vision. She published topics based on her personal life, including breast cancer, foster care, and adoption issues. When Rosie walked, a several-year legal battle ensued in which the publisher and Rosie sued one another for breach of contract. The judge ruled against both parties and ultimately dismissed the suit. But the damage was done. *Rosie,* formerly *McCall's,* went belly up and one of the original Seven Sisters took her last breath.

Then there were six.

THE REMAINING SIX SISTERS AT A GLANCE

Woman's Day: Craft ideas and home decorating

Family Circle: Parenting tweens and teens

Good Housekeeping: Anti-aging focus, health and fitness

Ladies' Home Journal: Work, marriage, health

Redbook: Working and married mothers

Better Homes & Gardens: Garden, home décor, and family

CAN GLOSSIES SURVIVE THE FUTURE?

Over the past thirty years, women's magazines have cycled in and out of recessionary periods where first TV, music, and movies, and later computers, cell phones, and the Internet drew women's attention away from the simple pastime of reading magazines. Our increasingly digitized world of new media and social networking suddenly demanded much more of our individual attention. Clicking and scrolling competed with the idle flipping of glossy pages, yet surprisingly, magazine circulation hasn't totally plummeted as a result. The problem was, and perhaps still is, that there is a perception among advertisers and the public that print magazines are going the way of the dinosaurs.

In fact, The Power of Print, an industry-wide magazine campaign erected by five powerhouse magazine publishers, launched a series of ads in national glossies to address this very issue in 2010. The ads used fun, friendly text and magazine titles as fill-in words to promote the vitality of magazines as a medium. A portion of one such ad reads:

> *Barely noticed amidst the thunderous Internet clamor is the fact that magazine readership has risen over the past five years. . . . What it proves . . . is that a new medium doesn't necessarily displace an existing one. Just as movies didn't kill radio. Just as TV didn't kill movies. An established medium can continue to flourish so long as it continues to offer a unique experience. And, as reader loyalty and growth demonstrate, magazines do.[27]*

Just as they did in the past, magazines today risk angering and disappointing their readers with content that arouses controversy, falls short of expectations, or fails to live up to reader's standards—like excessive airbrushing or celebrity profiles that come up short. Editors walk a fine line each month trying to put out content free of such scrutiny.

Readers Respond

"I was very angry about two years ago when *Ladies' Home Journal* ran an essay written by a woman who hated her family's cat and was happy when it got scared and ran off into a strange city while they were moving. Her thoughts were cruel and heartless. I never have—and never will—pick up an issue of *LHJ* again for publishing this selfish woman's glee over the demise of a poor scared animal. To think that they actually *paid* someone for such rubbish angers me."
—Sharon, training manager

Can women's magazines survive, even thrive in the future? History shows they have and they can, by revamping formats, revising content, redesigning layouts, adding and deleting essays, fiction, contests, columns, and advice. All the while, they play with the line between reality and fantasy, all to offer readers a unique experience they cannot find through other mediums. And how do they do this?

When a publisher decides a magazine must be rebranded, like *Redbook* experienced several times over the past decades, the entire staff has often been let go in favor of new blood with new ideas and a slew of new writers. New contributors are coveted, and landing an interview with the hottest celebrity can send one magazine's newsstand sales soaring, while another lags. The dance continues, tightening belts and paring down when times are lean, or assigning content to contributors with abandon and covering the latest trends, fads, and "gets" when times are fat.

Sure, the formula has changed depending on the decade, but women's magazines today still address their readers as women, slanting material through a female lens. And while investigative articles and in-depth analyses of political and social issues are shadows of their former pieces, and fiction is gone, victims of general

GLOSSY FACT

Today, all women's magazines are helmed by female editors, and an estimated 90 percent of editorial staff and contributors are women as well. While male editors and contributors still play a role, the male stamp is less visible today than ever before.[24]

interest magazines and twenty-four-hour cable news, what remains are informational glossies chock-full of advice on careers, home, and family. The magazines provide entertainment. They interpret things female, whether that be sex, fashion, or health. They exude intimacy and create a sisterhood among their readership. Sadly, the ugly side exists as well. Messaging that's damaging, airbrushed ideals of beauty and lifestyles, objectification of women, shallow topics, and misleading, even fear-mongering, content.

At their best, women's magazines are a space to be comforted, entertained, and advised, a place that is fun to visit. Women's glossies shine a light on us, and some may argue they dare to reveal our ideals, struggles, hopes, and dreams so that we can enrich our lives. Perhaps that's always been the goal of the women's magazine, no matter what the decade.

As long as readers believe they'll get something they need, want, or value out of the glossy magazines gracing the racks at the grocery store, they'll continue dropping them in their shopping bags.

Chapter 2

THE PINK GHETTO

A woman should be pink and cuddly for a man.
—Jayne Mansfield

You might have a spectacular salary with an office on the thirty-second floor, but if you're a woman working within the women's magazine industry, you're part of what's called the Pink Ghetto, albeit a figurative one. Coined in 1983 from a study of women and poverty in America, the term "pink ghetto" described traditional female, often low-paying jobs such as teachers, nurses, and secretaries.[1] Today, the term has been co-opted to describe any career that attracts more than a handful of women, which includes the hallowed halls of the lady-magazine industry, whose mastheads often only boast one or two token men.

What's really made the term stick, however, isn't the high ratio of women working in the industry so much as the content and style of women's magazines, and the culture in which they thrive. Whether it's the stereotype of catty work environments, the increasingly shallow fluff and false content, or the literal scenting of the pages, women's magazines today have largely earned the Pink Ghetto moniker. There are always exceptions to the rule, of course, and high points exist in the form of strong editorial campaigns. Here, we take a look at whether the catty culture of the women's mag industry is mere stereotype or if it falls somewhere in between. We'll also examine how magazines lure us in with their continued redesigns, yet send us running for cover from the scents that waft from between the pages, and whether readers are misled by the writers and editors working in this glossy ghetto.

DOES THE DEVIL WEAR PRADA?

Many writers and editors assert that working in the Pink Ghetto is like being in high-school: It's clicky, backstabbing, and hierarchical, largely due to the Queen Bee mentality among high-ranking editors. This culture was deliciously exaggerated in the 2006 movie *The Devil Wears Prada* (TDWP), in which the fictional editor-in-chief, played with perfect pitch by Meryl Streep, is presumably modeled after *Vogue* editor-in-chief Anna Wintour.[2] Streep's character is the epitome of snobbish disregard and catty bitchiness, hostile to underlings and viciously competitive. The lesser staffers who are portrayed in the movie are by degrees less loathsome than Streep's character, but they're nonetheless played off as part of the greater dysfunctional whole. The movie's a hoot, and while it's clearly more farce than fact, do women working within the Pink Ghetto really act like this? Well, it all depends on the magazine.

One former *Vogue* editor with whom I attended a conference mentioned that she found herself alone in the elevator with Wintour one day and tried to thank her for a box of expensive chocolates she and the other staff had received as a holiday gift. Instead of being gracious, Wintour looked demurely down her nose at the "lowly" associate editor, turned away, and stared at the elevator wall without uttering so much as a sound. The two rode the rest of the way in silence, the associate editor feeling embarrassed and firmly put in her place by having "deigned" to speak to Ms. Wintour.

"Jamie," a New York City writer, recounted her recent experience of being an intern at one of the top women's health magazines on the stands today. "The executive editor referred to me as 'Intern Jamie,'" she said. As in, when Jamie kicked in an opinion or spoke at an editorial meeting, the executive editor would say things like, "Thank you for weighing in, Intern Jamie," and, "We appreciate your thoughts, Intern Jamie." But her all-time favorite was, "You're here to learn, not to contribute, Intern Jamie."

Apparently, there does exist a mean-girl mentality at the top of some women's magazines.

Then there's the notorious case of "MagHag," an anonymous industry insider who blogged about the nefarious, very TDWP, shenanigans and attitudes of staff within the Pink Ghetto, at her blog, FourInchHeelsOnly.wordpress.com. In blog entry after blog entry, this anon-o-writer called out the insidious incidents that took place behind the scenes at various magazines and the women who dominated them, alleging that clothing labels were checked to make sure subordinates were wearing designer fashions, heels had to be at least four inches high, and editors took three-hour alcohol-filled lunches; interns and assistants were said to perform the kinds of tasks portrayed in the movie (running out to buy something for an editor's child), and editors were criticized for everything from their freebie beauty-closet goodies to the gaudy clothes they wore and bags they carried.[3]

Rumors in the women's magazine industry swirled about MagHag's identity, with reports that some staffers went so far as trying to match up editors whose sick days corresponded with blogposts in which MagHag said she was home ill. But in the end, Hag's blog petered out with nary a word about her identity, though most speculated that she was at one time employed at one of the top fashion rags.

And just like the title of the MagHag's blog, "Four Inch Heels Only," it's said that some very discriminating editors-in-chief require their staff to sport stilettos at work (though we wonder if an actual ruler is whipped out to make sure they measure up). In a May 2011 editorial letter in *Allure*, Editor-in-Chief Linda Wells commented that back in the day you used to be able to tell which women worked for which of Conde Nast's dozens of magazines when you sized them up in the elevator: Women who dressed demurely in skirts and twinsets worked at *Glamour*. Ones wearing shift dresses, pearls, and pumps worked at the *Brides* group of magazines; while women wearing silk, leather, and stilettos, later famously depicted as "clackers" in *The Devil Wears Prada,* edited beauty and fashion magazines like *Vogue*.[4]

Insider Input

"Most fashion people aim for uniqueness in all things, especially their appearance . . . And yet, so many of us are members of a tribe, our common markings as obvious as face paint. It's as if those high-school cliques—jocks, cheerleaders, geeks, and stoners—still have a hold on us."[5]
—Linda Wells, Editor-in-chief, *Allure* magazine

And in yet another letter from Wells, she points out that some of the most talented people she's ever worked with sported bad perms and ugly sweaters. These folks would likely be overlooked by other magazines who won't hire anyone overweight (yes, over size 6), or who isn't dressed impeccably—or yes, wearing heels—but Wells insists it's talent that counts, not heel height.

Having known and worked with dozens of editors at top women's glossies over the last fifteen years, I can say that the bad eggs are more exception than rule. For instance, for every editor that can't be bothered to answer a call from a lowly writer, there are dozens who happily meet writers for coffee, lunch, and in their busy offices, where, dare we note, they often sport flats for walking the New York City streets. Other editors I know even wear jeans to work because it's casual Friday and they're heading to a Mets game after work, or they have windblown hair and wear little makeup. They're also frazzled and overworked—as in, they eat lunch at their desk or just plain skip it some days. A former editor at *Ladies' Home Journal* takes the 7:00 PM train out of the city every night. And a *MORE* editor once mentioned that since they started their website, they all work 30 percent more than they used to. Doesn't sound like ladies who lunch for three hours, does it?

Despite the catty culture of some glossy hallways, there are countless smart, mature, creative women who work for women's magazines, many of whom are often dissatisfied with the product, the culture, and the focus of the writing. Many women's magazine writers and editors feel they don't get respect from general interest editors and also find it difficult to cross over into other more literary writing venues. Sadly, women's magazines, on the whole, win fewer national magazine awards. There's less room in the chick slicks for the lengthy narrative journalism that usually wins these prizes. And worse, when a smart women's magazine like *Cookie, Hallmark,* or *Lifetime* (all have ceased publication) enters the fray, it may not survive for very long. Seems the ghetto isn't always such a great place to be, pink or not.

Some editors are willing to take a risk on these startup publications, but as they relocate up the masthead chain, they often risk their very career. One editor left a major parenting magazine on what she said was "a wing and a prayer" to relocate to *Lifetime*, a magazine that was based on the channel of the same name, which consequently folded a short time later.

While it used to be considered a badge of esteem to work for the Seven Sisters, times have changed—as has content. Still, opportunities for good writing—and behavior!—continues. The Pink Ghetto is populated by dozens of women's glossies—from *O Magazine* and *Real Simple* to *Women's Health* and *Shape* magazine—offering more jobs for women writers and editors, but also more competition for readers within the ghetto. Nowadays, magazines struggle to set themselves apart from each other, either by appealing to a unique niche (such as *MORE,* which targets the over-forty demographic), or redesigning themselves using formulaic styles that made other magazines successful. No matter the direction, magazines will always reflect the sensibilities—or non-sense—of its editors, whether in the pages or out.

REDESIGNING A BEHEMOTH

Circulation and advertising revenue are the bread and butter of all women's magazines, so the battle to lure in both readers and advertisers is at the root of any game change in a magazine's design and editorial focus.

Thus, magazine publishers, under pressure from corporate owners to remain competitive within the glossy market, are continually trying to both please their loyal readers *and* attract new ones. To do this, they are endlessly making adjustments to magazines, ranging from major redesigns to what's known in the industry as "masthead massacres"—giving several editors, or sometimes the entire staff, the boot. (Ironically, although a new editor-in-chief or creative director might be eager to put her individual stamp on the revamped glossy, readers are likely to complain about it, if they even perceive the change to begin with.) Change, while necessary on the one hand, is also a risky endeavor on the other.

Sure, the editorial format can be jacked up and new columns added. The order of content can be rearranged, the sections renamed, the font size or cover shots may differ slightly from before, but nothing is ever as whole hog as a major redesign implies. That's too risky for business. Instead, the powers-that-be switch things up only slightly, like a magician's optical illusion. The reader thinks something looks different, somewhat altered from the previous incarnation, but if they squint their eyes just so, maybe not. And that's how the industry likes it: changed, but not really. In case you don't love the new spruce up, maybe you won't notice. And if you do like it, well, there you go—we improved it especially for you.

Insider Input

"Often the cover lines have very little to do with the actual stories, and even if they do, they've been sexed up."
—Lola Augustine Brown, writer

Take *Women's Health*. Prior to Editor-in-Chief Michele Promaulayko taking the helm in 2008, this magazine was packed with useful, humorous health and fitness information, along the lines of *Men's Health*. It had a kick-ass vibe and a sassy tone for readers in their twenties, thirties, and early forties who cared about all things healthy. Enter Promaulayko, formerly an editor at *Cosmo*, and *WH* embarked on a new footpath. The feminist website Jezebel refers to it as *Cosmo*-lite, saying, "Many writers and readers contend Promaulayko dumbed down health content, ramped up the beefcake, and added more beauty, celebs, and sex to the pages of *Women's Health* after taking the reins."[6]

Missing from the covers were the athletic models who were trim yet healthy looking, and in their place were the celebrity cover shots and retouched bikini-clad photos of the megafamous. Slashed also were the two- to three-page spreads of complex workouts in favor of small sketches of exercise moves and workout tips, often relegated to the bottom of the page. Prominent, however, were boatloads of sex information, like "The Better Sex Workout! Tighten, Tone, Then Mmmoan," and "Mattress Math Lessons." After taking the helm, Promaulayko appointed some former *Cosmo* cohorts, who clearly had the balls to bust out the new theme. Whereas *WH* previously covered one sexual health topic per issue, these articles were now numerous feature pieces splashed throughout the book.

With content like "Drop Two Dress Sizes in Two Weeks" (impossible unless you're stranded on a season of "Survivor") and "Why Newlyweds Cheat" (inspiring topic for the newly hitched), the magazine began to smack of a former hybrid of itself: health information coupled with *Cosmo's* notoriously loose moral code and exaggerated sex and health claims.

Then there was *Southern Living's* redesign in 2010. This book, which covered the lifestyle, culture, and trends of all things southern—from the best travel destinations and regional recipes to helpful tips on growing southern roses—epitomized southern living for over forty years. The once iconic seasonal covers—

orange pumpkins and gourds in October and the lavender lilacs in May—were replaced with covers of nothing particular below the Mason-Dixon Line.

Southern recipes petered out to a scant few, replaced by beauty, fitness, and fashion content—what every magazine unfortu-

---

Insider Input

"The whole *Cosmo*-ization of *Women's Health* still makes me angry. When this mag launched, it was amazing. It had interesting essays, useful nutrition information, and real exercises. Oh, and real athletes on the cover. Now this crap. Sad."

—Jen Miller, freelance journalist

---

nately thinks it needs to compete with and become a formulaic lady-mag. Now it looks like just another book, with a few southern destinations and recipes for pecan pie tossed in to anchor the title, surrounded by pieces on the fashions, fitness, and beauty trends the rest of the women's magazines *already* cover.

Of course, if sales are up or ad dollars soar, the redesign is considered a success, whether the design changes merit it or not. Yet sometimes a redesign comes along that raises the bar. Samir Husni, dubbed "Mr. Magazine" at the University of Mississippi's School of Journalism, touts a *Woman's Day* overhaul that he says rocked the typical revamp.

According to Husni, *WD* tackled a fixer-upper in 2007 when Editor-in-chief Jane Chesnutt was at the helm and several key elements and critical design features took root. One element lauded was the addition of a special opening page, or "splash page," for each section, which made navigation a breeze and readers feel welcomed, whether they first turned to the editor's note at the front of the book, an article midway in, or to the last page.[7]

Woman's Day delivered on its promises: "101 Ways to Save Money on Groceries" or "Ten Things you Must do for your Health Today." If you promise it within the pages, you must deliver the

---

Insider Input

"I do not believe in redesigns. I tell my clients all the time that magazines are not born for redesigns and face-lifts. Plastic surgery will not help. The best way for a magazine to succeed is to debut a 'new editorial platform' to keep up with the times."[8]

—Samir Husni, professor, University of Mississippi School of Journalism

---

information. And that doesn't always happen in women's glossies. Sometimes, what's promised on the cover or in the table of contents isn't always delivered in the accompanying article.

Other *WD* refurbishes included offering a bonus, or freebies, like recipe cards or clip-and-save information, such as how to do a breast self-examination. *Real Simple* is expert at this, providing content packed with useful websites we've never heard of, new ways to use common household items, and freebie alerts, like when an ice cream company is giving away free cones, or day spas across a certain region are offering discounted massages. The *Woman's Day* redesign also included adding perforated pull-out cards with recipes, lists of websites for shopping deals, or other

GLOSSY FACT

When it comes to content, magazines don't always deliver on what they promise. The October 2011 issue of *Health,* for example, includes the cover line, "Breast Cancer Cure you Must Know About." However, the inside article, which is titled "Breast Cancer: What you Must Know Now," only includes recent developments on treatment and drugs, not information on how breast cancer has been cured. Since, um, it hasn't been.

"bonus" materials thought to make reader's lives more convenient with pull-and-go information.

Another *WD* redesign change considered successful was grouping "like with like," though most magazines have had this trick down for decades. In other words, the food section is all together, the health articles fall within one segment in the middle or back of the book, the feel-good family stories are placed back-to-back rather than spread haphazardly throughout. If many of these traits were missing from previous manifestations of *WD*, perhaps that 2007 redesign constituted a successful new venture.

Redesigns aren't always for the stodgy Sisters, either. How about *Seventeen,* the ubiquitous teenybopper slick that's been showing teen girls how to talk to boys and apply blush correctly for decades? In 2011, advertisers bumped up designer merchandise placements from, say, things that teenagers might actually afford if they save up for them—like a new iPod—to $400 Coach bags and $300 designer denims instead. Yup, the babysitting biz must be booming if the powers-that-be thought their readers could afford the designer digs and trend-setting accessories showcased monthly. That or they think the majority of their teenage reader's parents have incomes to knockout the requisite Coach bag and Marc Jacob wedges on a back-to-school shopping spree.

Seventeen Editor-in-Chief Ann Shoket believed that after years of recessionary belt-tightening, her readers were ready to start splurging again. "We 100 percent do not want to alienate our readers who want to shop at accessible price points," she said in an article for *Adweek*.[9] Yet it was widely bantered in magazine circles whether such a move would endear readers or send them running to other teen magazines. In fact, magazine content in general, including the price of the items showcased, greatly influences whether readers will loyally support a magazine, and any change that rubs readers the wrong way is fodder for lost sales.

WHAT A GIRL WANTS (IN A MAGAZINE)

The women's magazine ghetto was and is all about service. Where to buy the trendiest new bag is as much a staple as the how-to-do-everything-better pieces, from communicating with your sullen teen and slowing the pesky signs of aging to reorganizing your closet and handling your man's balls correctly during oral sex (yup, an actual *Cosmo* story). Unfortunately, the advice that can make us sing with a new flourless chocolate torte recipe or soar with ten sure-fire tips to blow his mind in the bedroom comes with the message that our lives need fixing. Magazines blast us with cover lines that presume we need self-improvement, that we're not good enough as is, but we can be if we read the articles and advice within their pages.

Monthly how-to staples, like saving your marriage or getting your kids to do chores, echo that same message of inadequacy. Men's magazines, on the other hand, rarely lead with lines and topics that assume men are saddled with shortcomings—like how to compensate for a small penis or tips for blasting that pesky beer belly, once and for all. Nope, most men's magazines come from the presumption that male readers are at the top of their game, and they deserve to be entertained and enlightened, so here are all the hot celebrity women, trends, tech gadgets, and travel adventures you'll find interesting. Many men's magazines (think *Maxxim* and *GQ*) are unapologetically sexist, to be sure, which presents its own knotty issues about messaging, but even the least chauvinist among them (*Men's Journal,* for example) share a common purpose: they're a *respite* for their male readers, a distraction from their stress and real-life shortcomings, great reading material to peruse while on the john: In other words, they entertain and enlighten, not criticize.

GLOSSY FACT

See if you can spot the disparity in the messages being sent via the cover lines of two magazines that have a similar editorial focus but appeal to different genders:

March 2012 *Men's Health:* "Lean, Fit & Fast," and "Iron Abs"

March 2012 *Women's Health:* "The #1 Health Risk for Fit Women" and "Erase Zits & Wrinkles"

Not always the case with women's magazines. Here, we're turning out a generation of young women who may just misconstrue women's magazines as gospel and begin their self-improvement programs of, say, losing weight or avoiding wrinkles as early as their teens, using needles and knives to become a better-looking teen or twentysomething (more on this ugly trend in chapters 5 and 6). It seems asinine to worry about growing old when you're still young or live in a culture where if you aren't hovering near anorexia, you're likely overweight. Never mind that size 10, 8, even 6, for God's sake, is classified as "plus size" in the modeling world, where anyone who can't fit into the size 0–2 sample clothes displayed in magazine fashion spreads and print ads probably needs a diet. While women are seeking to become self-empowered with the wisdom and advice imparted within the content of the magazines' pages, it's painful to think we must be perfect all the time.

For example, in the July 2011 issue of *Self*, reader inspiration Jennifer Davis dropped twenty pounds. Unfortunately, she went from 125 to 106 pounds, looking clearly anorexic in her smiling photo. What a dangerous and screwed up ideal to promote: that the thin should strive to be thinner. Seeing both the numbers and the photo, the editor that okayed Davis as the weight-loss reader inspiration ought to consider the unhealthy ideal *Self* is promoting.

But chick slicks weren't always a medium for shallow fluff or airbrushed ideals, nor were their readers looking for that. Many of the earlier women's magazines, such as *Delineator* and *Pictorial Review*, were once deemed thought-provoking, literary, and political. They didn't talk down to women, nor did they harangue us to improve our lives. Once upon a time, the foremothers of our contemporary women's glossies birthed the serialized monthly story, with contributors like Edith Wharton and Upton Sinclair. They included poetry and short stories, service articles, and features on social issues. In today's terms, we'd say it was "cool" to be reading those nineteenth-century magazines. Back then, we'd feel smart. Now women almost apologize for slumming in the Pink Ghetto, referring to their *Cosmo* fix or *Real Simple* addiction as a "guilty pleasure." When did the glossy page come to represent a double dose of guilt, anyway? Similar to the reality TV craze, we now mumble under our breath in mortification if anyone knows we spent the evening watching *The Jersey Shore, Real Housewives of Anywhere*, or *The Kardashians* lest someone think our penchant for fluff, cheese, and sleaze TV makes us any less of a woman. Like these shows, the chick slicks may be considered just another embarrassing dumbed-down reality in our lives, and we know it. We know that, for the most part, magazines are often selling us swampland in the desert, but we still embark, drawn in by the catchy headlines and the promise that we'll get what we're searching for, be it advice, ideas, inspiration, or entertainment. Sure, they may be cheesy, but we read them anyway.

On the positive side, women's magazine stories can be both educational and investigative, exposing women's issues and covering politics that the mainstream media tend to avoid (see more on this in chapter 9). For instance, *Ms.* magazine is credited with

Readers Respond

"Reading magazines is like eating a candy bar or a bag of chips you know you should put down. Sickeningly sweet or salty, but oh-so-satisfying!"
—Nicole, public relations professional

coining the term "battered woman," catapulting domestic abuse and violence against women to the forefront. *Ms.*, which first used the term in a 1976 cover story on abused women, became the first national magazine to address the issue, even including a photo of a woman's bruised and battered face on the cover.[10] The lifesaving Pink Ribbon Campaign, which today is part of our cultural lexicon, was first introduced in the pages of *Self* magazine when it joined with the Estée Lauder Company in 1992 to help raise awareness of breast cancer and increase funding for breast cancer research. The campaign—which continues to raise funds to fight breast cancer—was actively supported and publicized by all magazines in the Pink Ghetto in an unparalleled example of the collective power women's magazines can have, if properly directed. What's more, thanks to *Woman's Day* teaming up with the American Heart Association in 2004 for its annual Red Dress Awards, it's likely that every woman in America who's ever read a chick slick now knows that heart disease is the leading killer of women.

Sadly, however, lung cancer kills more women than breast cancer, yet isn't afforded anywhere near the coverage devoted to the Pink Ribbon Campaign. Why is that? Isn't the top cancer killer of women worthy of the same coverage given to these other diseases? Why not a Black Lung Campaign, complete with black ribbons and black dresses signifying women's lungs dying off at an increased rate? In the 1980s, and perhaps early 1990s, the reason might have been a complex dance between editors and advertising folks. If women's books were running cigarette ads, for instance— which they were at the time—wouldn't tobacco companies object to article content that not only told women that smoking was bad for their health, but worse, that it could also lead to the most terrible and deadliest cancer among women—a fact that was widely supported by research and medical professionals at the time?

You betcha.

Sure, the glossies occasionally cover smoking cessation. They also make good on including advice on ways to ditch smokes as a way to improve your cholesterol levels and reduce your risk for certain cancers—like lung, throat, and mouth cancer—yet the disease is not given the same attention as other deadly diseases among women.

GLOSSY FACT

"Women's magazines' juxtaposition of tobacco ads with antismoking information may weaken the potentially powerful health messages the magazines' editors seem to want to convey. One page warns readers about the perils of smoking; the next promotes cigarettes. The hypocrisy of magazines' advocating healthy lifestyles while continuing to advertise cigarettes compromises not only the health of America's women, but the credibility of their favorite magazines."[11]

—The American Council on Science and Health, 1999

Sadly, women in their fifties and sixties who are being diagnosed with lung cancer, emphysema, and chronic obstructive pulmonary disease (COPD) likely read the glossies back in the '60s and '70s. During that era, magazines all but glamorized and promoted smoking, if by no other means than running ads in which sexy, smart, hip women lit up on the page. Remember Virginia Slims ads? Worse, some magazine's editors balked when approached about ditching tobacco advertisers. After all, consider the millions of dollars in ad revenue that would be lost!

Take *Glamour* Editor-in-Chief, Cynthia Leive. In 2007, she responded to California Congresswoman Lois Capps' open letter that asked women's magazines to voluntarily stop cigarette advertising. She noted that her magazine repeatedly ran warning articles about the dangers of smoking, citing an August 2007 feature, "The #1 Cancer Killing Young Women and How to Beat It," but added "that smoking remained a personal choice and the Camel ads in question were legal."[12]

Today, tobacco companies no longer advertise in women's magazines. In June 2000, Philip Morris announced it would voluntarily pull cigarette ads from forty-two magazines that were still running the ads. It took another six years for RJ Reynolds to follow. In 2007, they also voluntarily pulled tobacco ads from magazines, thanks to pressure from public health organizations and Congress—not from women's magazines.

While we're on the subject of insidious content, how about the "real women" that are presented in the pages of the Pink Ghetto? Are they real? Take a closer look.

THE "SOURCES" OF THE PINK GHETTO

As trusting readers, we generally assume that editorial content in magazines is written with journalistic integrity—even when it's fluff—and that the quotes, the scenarios, and especially the women used as sources in these stories are as real as the laundry that piles up in our hampers every week. Well, here's the truth of it: maybe not.

In general, women's magazines rely on what are called "composite characters" to anchor some stories or put anecdotes and sidebars together. She is a distillation of a bunch of real women who were interviewed on the street or in cities across the country for the article, refined to fit the "ideal" woman the editor wants for that story or feature. They're called composites because editors may take out information that is disconcerting, like her age or sexual orientation, if it doesn't fit the angle of the story, and instead offer up only the information the magazine wants the reader to know, like her weight loss methods or how many times a week she gets busy; details that fit precisely into the package they've created. For instance, for an article on how women drop five pounds for a big event, editors may solicit a variety of women with this question. Their answers, however, are distilled into what the editor's vision and premise of the story has become. Say their angle is to show the desperate things women might do to lose weight. They won't include a sensible answer like cutting back on fatty snacks because that doesn't fit the angle; or the editor might change it up to read that the woman cuts back on breakfast, the most important meal of the day—which fits the "desperate" hook. It may smack of phoniness, like reading about a married woman who claims she has sex every day. Readers *almost* can't buy it, but they can't put their finger on why. They assume they're being given the truth here. A more discerning or cynical reader might balk or snort and say, "Yeah, sure, *that's* a stretch. . . but it's *true,* at least to some degree, right?" Well, depends on how you define truth, since it's the truth the *magazine* wants you to know. Sometimes, magazines get lucky. After all, it takes only one woman out of perhaps dozens interviewed to support the point the magazine's trying to make. Perhaps there *is* a married woman out there who falls outside the norm and does have sex every day, for better or worse (depending on the spouse!). That one response is all they need to make their case.

In a 2009 Huffington Post piece titled "Why Magazines Suck," freelance magazine writer Alison Stein Wellner writes:

> *I've just ended a relationship with a certain magazine, whose name I won't reveal, but who I've written for several times in the past. They wanted a story about how women with certain Bad Disease found their lives changed by the illness. Sounds reasonable enough. The process is this: I am to go out and find a number of women with this Bad Disease and talk to them about how their lives have changed. I am given various storylines by the editors: 'My distant marriage has been made closer.' 'Bad Disease made her fearless in the face of a relationship that used to terrify her.' 'She embraced alternative treatments, but not too much, so she doesn't seem like a wacko,' etc. These are storylines dreamed up in an editorial meeting. They are invented. They are fiction. My job is to then talk to as many women—real breathing women—as possible to find someone that conforms to these storylines. I am asked to provide photos. If the woman has an undesirable quality—like, say, she's a lesbian—she's disqualified.[13]*

Dozens of assignments similar to this are commissioned to writers each month in the women's magazines on various topics. Stories abound from women writers I know who have found their quotes routinely rewritten, their stories "tweaked," and fact-checking apathetic at best at a few of these mags; nonexistent at others where those real women (composites) are in the mix, or within any topic having to do with sex, relationships, or where men are involved. For example, a *Cosmo* editor speaking on a panel of editors once said that quotes are rewritten to sound as perky as the rest of the copy because no one really talks like that. It's common knowledge among writers that when real women's anecdotes aren't juicy enough at some of these publications, they're revamped to read more racy or raunchy. And since last names aren't used, the composite of a women in Middle America who speaks of, say, the hottest place she's ever done the deed are juiced up appropriately by the editing powers-that-be—if the women even exist at all.

Insider Input

"I busted my butt getting quotes from real women for a dieting story in a magazine well known for changing them up. When I saw the story in print, the quotes were changed, the last names of the women I spoke to were left off, even their ages were altered."
—Ann, writer

Even at the magazines that are horrified that some of these practices take place (and they are numerous too), they nonetheless assign articles to writers that require them to search for sources that fit certain parameters; say, women between the ages of twenty-two and thirty-six who admit their sex life is supercharged or their mate has kinky quirks. Or maybe it's someone who's lost ten pounds or eats nothing but a raw diet, or someone whose spouse left her for a younger version, or who sleeps with guys on the first date.

Magazines require women to be geographically diverse, so they may need someone on the East Coast, someone from Middle America, and a West Coaster. They may want a specific version of a woman's story, say one who has been diagnosed with a certain disease in the past year who hasn't had conventional treatment for it, but followed a naturopathic approach or used some little-known Eastern remedy. Essentially, the editors invent the story—its trends and angles—then they send a writer out on assignment to find people to shoehorn into their stories. The real stories of women in the magazine articles? Not so much. But even if these stories reek of bullshit, they're offset sweetly by perfumed pages.

THE SCENT OF THE GHETTO

In the constant battle to distinguish themselves in the Pink Ghetto, magazines have found creative ways to lure in readers and advertisers. One clever and highly successful endeavor has been to include perfume samples, or scent strips, in every issue. It's no wonder that magazines are often referred to as the "perfumed pages." Not only did adding these strips take pressure off the editorial department to come up with a freebie (like links to product deals, pull-out cards, or helpful websites, as mentioned earlier), but magazines were only too happy to oblige advertisers who wanted to include a scent strip with their latest perfume ads, since it came at no cost to the magazine. Nice deal. Plus, scientific studies show scent can sweeten pleasant feelings, reduce anxiety, change perception, and trigger memory and desire—presumably instilling positive associations with magazines.[14] In fact, 75 percent of our emotions are generated by what we smell, and since branding is all about building emotional ties between product and consumer, it's a no-brainer that the women's magazine industry would include scent to entice you to the products they're selling. In the past decade, innovators have expanded on the original strip technology, introducing fragrance in many creative ways.

GLOSSY FACT

A Roper Starch survey found that scented ads increase readership by 136 percent.[15] Another study by *The New York Times* found that 81 percent of consumers would choose a product they could see and smell over one that they could only see.[16] By mid-2007, both *The Wall Street Journal* and *USA Today* began including scented ads, and since the first quarter of 2008, fragrance strips have popped up in most major magazines.

So just how does this sniffapalooza come to pass on the page? Scented ads for perfume are coated with tiny capsules that contain the fragrance. This itsy-bitsy smell technology can only be seen with a microscope. The capsules are made of a delicate plastic that breaks easily when rubbed or scratched. The technique is known as *microencapsulation*. The capsules are affixed to the paper to prevent the scents from bursting during rough handling. Once the ad is ripped open, the scent wafts upward, or you can rub the strip across your sexiest pulse points for a quick pick-me-up.

The process of microencapsulation has been used for decades in those fun Scratch 'n Sniff promotions many of us discovered in the '70 and '80s. Today's technology is designed to release a scent only after being touched by the reader. Perfume manufacturers mix the perfume essence with water, then use a machine with a fine nozzle to spray water droplets on to the paper. The droplets are then covered with a thin plastic sheet or sticky covering. When the reader rubs a finger on the highlighted portion of the page or opens the equivalent of the fragrance sticky note, the protective plastic coating breaks and releases a whiff of the perfume.

Add three or four of these fragrant bombs to a book, and the entire magazine simply reeks. Typically, the fragrance odors escape from scented ads when the adhesive seals fail to stick or opens unintentionally.

Readers Respond

"I hate, hate, HATE them. They give me headaches, and I feel like I reek of them hours later, like I've been fragrance hijacked or something. I didn't *choose* to smell like your crappy fragrance, but now I can't scratch my face without gagging."
—Alyson, writer

Of course, not everyone loves to be assaulted with fragrance. In fact, for some people who are highly allergic to perfumes (of which there are quite a few), brushing up against a broken capsule of fragrance sends them to the medicine cabinet with an itchy, red rash, or they are nauseated after coming in contact with the magazine. Worse, the heady smell can trigger a migraine or an asthma attack.

In 1990, the fragrance industry faced lawsuits from consumers claiming they suffered allergic reactions to the scented pages in magazines. By 1995, the scented ads were encapsulated so they had to be activated to be smelled, and most magazines limited the number of ads per issue while a few refused to place scent strips.

Women in the lawsuit reported not being able to subscribe to women's magazines because of the fragrances, or they needed others to remove them before reading. Problem was, simply removing the strips did not eliminate the lingering odor.

But fragrance insiders report that half the perfume sold between Thanksgiving and Christmas may be attributed to these pungent magazine scent strips, and many magazines view the ads as revenue boosters year round, despite some reader's claims of despising them.[17]

Magazine and fragrance execs know they haven't heard the last of this issue. And almost all of the magazines have recently begun to offer scent-free copies to readers who request them, but few magazines publicize this policy.

A browse through the May 2011 issue of *Marie Claire* found three such smelly ads: Prada, the new eau de toilette; L'eau d'Issey Pour Homme by Issey Miyake; and Euphoria from Calvin Klein. Instructions on the scent strip include, respectively; "Lift here," "Lift and discover L'eau d'Issey Florale," and "Experience Euphoria Eau de Parfum."

Similarly, the May 2011 *Glamour* magazine carried scent strips from Acqua Di Gio by Giorgio Armani, Burberry Brit, and Very Irresistible Givenchy L'Intense. Interestingly enough, other perfume manufacturers advertised in this issue minus the fragrant-laden ads. They included Flora by Gucci, Pleasures by Estee Lauder, Coco Mademoiselle by Chanel, Infusion d'Iris by Prada, Espirit D'Oscar by Oscar de la Renta, Love by Chloe, and

Peace Love by Juicy Couture. So it seems it is possible to advertise fragrance without smelling it. And at least *Glamour* is limiting their fragrant load to three. Though truth be told, a quick rifling through the pages with thumb and forefinger and the sheets of brand new, unbroken fragrant scent-strips still give off a perfumy haze without so much as having to disturb the ads.

Lest you think fragrance is an issue in women's magazines only, that is hardly the case. General interest magazines and even men's books have jumped on the smell wagon and have loaded down their pages with a mix of musky manly odor, too. The May 2011 issue of *Men's Health* included Burberry Brit scent for men, and Ralph Lauren's Big Pony collection—a collage of four men's fragrances in a two-page smell spread that offered men the option of scents based on their personality or activities, according to the accompanying photos. Without breaking the capsules on these scent ads, scratching, or even touching the ad pages, *Men's Health* reeked of a college frat house on sorority sister night.

In April 1990, the U.S. Postal Service passed a regulation stating that "a fragrance advertising sample is nonmailable unless

the sample meets the following requirement: It must be sealed, wrapped, treated, or otherwise prepared in a manner reasonably designed to prevent individuals from being unknowingly or involuntarily exposed to the sample."[20] In other words, this is why half the chick slicks women subscribe to arrive sealed in landfill-busting plastic baggies.

In 1992, the California state government expanded the concept of that rule by passing a regulation that said, "Any fragrance advertising insert contained in a newspaper, magazine, mailing, or other periodically printed material shall contain only micro-encapsulated oils. Glue tabs or binders shall be used to prevent premature activation of the fragrance advertising insert."[21] Despite being a seemingly trivial issue, magazine fragrance strips spark debate and rancor among some readers, requiring laws, mailing regulations, and studies to deal with their smelly wrath.

. . .

Regardless of the scent of the magazine they subscribe to, readers simply expect—even crave—the truth from the Pink Ghetto.

Whether editors wear pearls or stilettos, reek of eau de toilette or ink, or tout campaigns that never quite take off, this ghetto should and must produce glossies full of useful stories, free of secret agendas, that include pertinent service advice and even-handed, well-researched issues that matter to readers. If the ghetto could quit turning home and decorating magazines into hybrids of the fashion or health rags, or health publications into oversexed versions of themselves because they believe women want to read about all these topics rolled into one heap of dried pulp, they may just be surprised by the devoted readers they attract.

Chapter 3

TRUTH IN ADVERTISING

*Most women's magazines simply try to mold women
into bigger and better consumers.*
—Gloria Steinem

Women's magazines are packed with articles promising readers that if they lose weight, look younger, or "improve" themselves in some other way, they can have it all—the perfect love life, well-behaved kids, great sex, *and* a rewarding career. No problem! As if slimmer thighs and thicker hair will get you a man *and* a corner office. But the messaging doesn't stop there. These so-called self-help pieces—which are monthly staples in every chick slick—are surrounded by advertisements for the myriad must-have products required to reach these goals. Coincidence? Not a chance. The placement of editorial content and advertising is as premeditated as a covert CIA operation.

To stay afloat, all women's magazines depend on the advertising dollars of fashion and beauty products. Even magazines typically thought of as our mother's and grandmother's magazines, like *Good Housekeeping*, which was so named to cover the cleaning, decorating, and homemaking skills every good wife and mother needed to possess, showcases ads of clothes, creams, bags, and shoes. Often they are pricey, and worse, they are placed strategically throughout the glossies to lure readers to splurge on items the magazine articles suggest they need. Read a magazine piece on how to stave off the effects of sun damage, how to drop a few pounds before swimsuit season, or the ten must-have closet staples, and notice how close they are to ads for antiaging creams, weight loss supplements, and a shoe designer.

It's an insidious relationship, and the success of both magazine and advertiser is dependent on manipulating you, the trusting reader, into obeisance to them. Thus, rather than run articles about the wisdom of "Eating for Nutrition, Not Narcissism" or "Embracing Your Imperfect Ass," magazines find seemingly friendly ways to undermine your sense of well-being by running articles that promise simple ways to overcome difficult-to-achieve standards of beauty and lifestyle, while taunting you with slim young models in advertisements that beckon you with sure-fire fixes.

Consider this: according to a Media Awareness Network article called "Beauty and Body Image in the Media," researchers report that "chick slicks have ten times more ads and articles promoting weight loss than men's magazines do, and over three-quarters of the covers of women's magazines include at least one message about how to change your body or appearance—by diet, exercise, beauty products, or cosmetic surgery."[1] It's no wonder the beauty and diet industries are booming. (Their profits range from forty to one hundred billion dollars each year, people.)

Bottom line: magazines need advertisers to stay afloat, and advertisers need magazines to sell products. It's a simple case of you scratch my back and I'll scratch yours, but at your expense.

Worse, research indicates that "exposure to images of too-thin, too-perfect, airbrushed female bodies are linked to depression, loss of self-esteem, and the development of unhealthy eating habits in women and girls, yet thin, young models and celebrities are favored by advertisers."[2] And according to the research group Anorexia Nervosa and Related Eating Disorders, "one out of every four college-aged women uses unhealthy methods of weight control—including fasting, skipping meals, excessive exercise, laxative abuse, and self-induced vomiting."[3] The pressure to be thin also affects young girls. The Media Awareness study cites a 2003 *Teen* magazine survey reporting that 35 percent of girls six to twelve years old have been on at least one diet, and that 50 to 70 percent of normal-weight girls believe they are overweight.[4]

When you couple these sad facts with data showing that advertisers and editors think women who are insecure about themselves are more likely to buy beauty products, accessories, clothing, and diet aids, then you can see a disturbing agenda behind the friendly

GLOSSY FACT

In 2011, the U.K.'s Advertising Standards Agency (ASA) banned L'Oreal advertisements featuring Julia Roberts and supermodel Christy Turlington for being "overly airbrushed." L'Oreal admitted the images were digitally manipulated and retouched, but denied they were misleading. The company insisted they "accurately illustrated" the effects of their products, and that the image of Roberts, taken by celebrity photographer Mario Testino, was an "aspirational picture."[5]

product taglines and go-girl dieting-advice articles that appear monthly in the glossy pages of women's magazines.

Of course, from time to time, efforts to buck these trends take place within the magazine industry. Women's glossies occasionally forgo retouching a photo or proffer up the before and after picture of some gutsy celebrity so readers can see what's been lobbed, swiped, washed out, or erased by a computerized retouching tool (more on this in chapter 5). Some magazines have been bold enough to showcase curvier models or actresses or claim that they "strive" to showcase women with real bodies, like when *Cosmo* put Adele on its December 2011 cover instead of the usual waifs. Unfortunately, despite the praise letters that pour into magazines when they pull back the curtain or buck trends, the magazine usually reverts back to its former practice of showcasing thin, flawless women's images by the next issue.

Sometimes, it's the advertisers who take the lead, all but forcing magazines to face the issue. The most prominent and far-reaching effort, of course, is the Dove Campaign for Real Women, which launched its own crusade against extreme ideals by portraying more realistic women with ordinary body types in its beauty product advertisements, using catchy taglines like "real

Readers Respond

"I love the Dove ads. Every time I pass a billboard, I honestly feel happier about myself. I think, *These are real, beautiful women; These are my friends.* I feel empowered and motivated. I feel like, 'Hey, I'm okay!'"
—Ann, mother and court reporter

women have curves." Yet despite the campaign's huge success and the positive feedback of readers and industry leaders alike, few advertisers have followed suit.

Other efforts are much more far-reaching, forcing the fashion, advertising, and magazine industry to be more accountable. After twenty-one-year-old Brazilian top model Ana Carolina Reston died in 2006 of anorexia, weighing eighty-eight pounds, the international industry did attempt to implement changes.

Madrid, one of the world's largest fashion meccas, took a stand against the anorexic ideal in 2006 by banning ultrathin models from the runway. In France, a bill that makes it illegal for anyone, including the fashion industry, advertisers, and websites to publicly incite extreme thinness was passed, and Spain recently developed a project with the aim of standardizing clothing

GLOSSY FACT

Mascara ads showing Kate Moss sporting "traffic-stopping" eyelashes were banned after complaints that the supermodel's lashes were false. The magazine and TV ads for Rimmel claimed that MagnifEyes Mascara produced 70 percent more lift with its unique vertical lift brush that helps wearers get the "London look." The Advertising Standards Authority investigated complaints that the lashes were false and challenged Rimmel to back up their claim that the mascara provided 70 percent more lift. Ad firm J Walter Thompson (JWT) claimed Moss was not wearing false eyelashes, but couldn't produce any evidence to back the claim. The firm fessed up that the lashes were [digitally] enhanced after the shoot. Because of lack of evidence, the ASA concluded that the images of the eyelashes in the ads may have exaggerated the benefits of the product.[7]

sizes by using a unique process in which a laser beam measures women's bodies to find the truest standardized measurement.[6]

Despite these inroads, advertisers still rule the magazine marketplace, and if you flip through any woman's magazine today, it's clear that when it comes to beauty, clothing, and lifestyle advertisements, being young, thin, and flawless is still in.

Yet despite this "beauty in advertising" trend, most discerning women readers have learned to take advertising with a grain of salt. We may even be used to ads that take poetic license with products, exaggerating the benefits of mascara or the arousing effects of the latest perfume. Uberbeauty and Barbie doll proportions have become the norm and seem to be part of the magazine advertisement game. Further, some women may even believe they're immune to the ads that appear around the articles they read. But as mentioned before, ad placement is strategic (more on this in the next section), and at one time, it was even guaranteed by contract between the magazine and the advertiser—yes, *contract*. And whether we *believe* we're being influenced or not, the messaging is nonetheless subliminal. For example, an ad for Oil of Olay Regenerist Firming Night Cream might appear near a celebrity profile of, say, Diane Keaton, in which the writer lauds Keaton's youthful appearance in the article. In the February 2012 issue of *Glamour*, a one-page beauty article titled "Emma Watson Knows her Beauty Stuff" depicts the Harry Potter starlet surrounded by her favorite lipstick, rouge, moisturizer, and perfume. The page immediately before and directly after the one-page article are advertisements for Revlon, featuring Emma Stone of the hit movie *The Help*, first surrounded by dozens of Revlon's lipstick shades and then hawking Revlon's Weightless Foam Foundation. The Emma Watson piece in the middle could just as easily be an ad; the Emma Stone ads surrounding the article could just as easily be editorial content. Which Emma is which? Which one is the ad; which one is the article?

We can't remember either.

To prove subliminal messaging exists, one Harvard study had subjects play a computer game where they were exposed to a series of words shown for a few thousandths of a second at a time.

Even though the words flashed by too quickly to be noticed, subjects' brains still registered their effect. People who were shown words like "wise," "astute," and "accomplished" walked from the study room significantly faster than those who saw the words "senile," "dependent," and "diseased."[8] Subliminal advertising slips by our self-awareness undetected, so our decisions are less informed and our guards don't even know they should be up.

Readers Respond

"I think advertising is an important part of the content—often more interesting and readable than the stuff offered up by the editors."
—Jennie, writer and editor

Today, we may expect more transparency from our favorite magazines or even from the brands we like and buy regularly, but the relationship between advertising and editorial has always been deeply purposeful.

WHAT'S WRONG WITH THIS AD PICTURE?

Aside from the mixed messaging that editorial content and ads can promote, there is another subtle play at misdirection that some magazines employ, and while it seems innocuous enough in its impact on readers, it's a terrific example of the coy interplay between magazines and advertisers, at the reader's expense.

On the inside cover of many women's magazines today, the editors share the inside scoop of what went on during the photo shoot of their celebrity cover model. The breezy piece might include the iTunes songs they played during the photo shoot, the food they ordered in, quaint or interesting facts about the location they shot in, and a personal tidbit or two about the celebrity, like how Kelly Ripa or Faith Hill arrived with hair in ponytail, wearing torn jeans and Keds, sans makeup, and carrying a box of donuts she thoughtfully brought for the crew. What the editor *doesn't* reveal, however, is that when the stylist gets around to doing the cover model's makeup and hair, she selects whatever products she wants to use, and editors later match up credits to please advertisers. Her pink cheeks?

GLOSSY FACT

In 2011, the U.K.'s Advertising Standards Authority (ASA) took yet another cosmetic company to task for false advertising. This time they targeted a L'Oreal Paris ad featuring the forty-one-year-old Rachel Weisz. The problem product? Revitalist Repair 10, which claims to target ten signs of aging. But Weisz's complexion was apparently too pristine—as in soft, glowing, and perfect. The ASA believed the image must have been altered substantially to make her complexion appear so smooth and even, and concluded that the cream's promised results were exaggerated and misleading.[9]

On an ironic side note, they also examined a similar L'Oreal Paris ad with Jane Fonda but found that Jane really did look that great!

Why that's Revlon's Sun-Kissed Glow blush! Her lush coral lips? Maybelline's Pinkalicious. The styling solution that makes her hair so shiny and bouncy? That's Garnier Fructis Sleek & Shine Anti-Frizz Serum. Or is it?

Have you ever gone to the makeup counter and tried to snag a palette of blush or tube of lipgloss you saw on the cover celeb? If you have, perhaps you didn't love it the way you thought you would. It just didn't look as amazing on you as it did on, say, Kate Winslet or Katie Holmes or Kate Middleton, the Princess of Wales. *Hmmm.* Disappointed, you probably assumed the problem was *you*. But the real reason the color fell short of expectation was because those gosh darn beauty editors did the best they could to match up the color used in a photo shoot with a color you can buy in the store. They are not one in the same. It's just never going to be exactly the right shade because it's simply not the same product, and that's why you didn't love the way it looked on you.

So much for truth in advertising.

The fact is, this little bait and switch is part and parcel of the women's magazine ad game. Here, advertisers and editors play nicey-nice and editors throw their best advertisers a bone by proffering up a few top-notch products in one of these "what is the celebrity wearing now" moments. The reality is, makeup artists use their own personal makeup palettes. There may be a couple of consumer name brands thrown in to their mix, but makeup artists generally make decisions about what to use based on their preferences and the needs of the shoot. They may blend, mix, and combine colors with the creative intention of Picasso, so a cheek color or an eye shadow may actually be the combination of four different shades of creams, gels, powders, and mineral makeup.

What's more, colors are changed and adjusted several times over to get just the right glow for the camera and the lighting conditions.

And if all the mixing and layering of texture and color doesn't work, the makeup artist will adjust, blend, and soften for the desired effect, if not swipe it all away and start over. Who knows what cosmetics end up on the celebrity!

Bottom line: rarely is the celebrity's lip color or eye shadow going to be a single product you'll find at Walgreens or at the Macy's makeup counter. That is fiction. Hell, the beauty editors may not even have attended the photo shoot. They were back at their desk, working on something else.

Instead, after the photo shoot is finished, they pore over the cover photo and match the colors that appear on the celeb's face to a close enough looking stand-in for what's available over the counter, or what their advertisers would like them to mention. It may be a product they've pulled from their sample beauty closet that's sitting on their desk right that minute. Plus, advertisers want—or even expect—those mentions. So whose makeup is most likely to be written in to that inside scoop? It's anybody's guess. There's no question that editors get close to the colors used on the celebrity, but their selections are often skewed to fit only the interests of their best advertisers—a small wink to their loyalty and ad-dollar largesse.

But this ad game isn't new; ad folk have had enormous influence on magazine editors since the very first glossies. In fact, some early magazines were created with the sole purpose of supporting product advertising, with editorial features added as a secondary element to draw the reader in.

ADS AND ARTICLES IN BED TOGETHER!

Ever since *Ladies' Magazine* debuted in 1828, editorial copy for women has been influenced by something other than reader's desires. There were no ads at this time, yet there was another influence the women's magazine editors had to consider: husbands. "Husbands may rest assured that nothing found in these pages shall cause her [his wife] to be less assiduous in preparing for his reception or encourage her to 'usurp station' or encroach upon prerogatives of men," wrote Sarah Josepha Hale, editor-in-chief of *Ladies'* at the time.[10] Hale went on to edit *Godey's Lady's Book* and avoided controversial topics of the day, such as slavery, abolition, and women's suffrage, lest men get their boxers in a wad over the content of what their wives were reading.

But real ads did eventually appear, starting with Butterick sewing patterns and newly available "health remedies" like pain relievers, mouthwashes, antiseptic creams, tinctures, and feminine hygiene products, helping to morph women's magazines into the catalogs they are today.

For the first time, women could actually purchase (either at local stores or directly through the magazine) what the magazines

GLOSSY FACT

Early ads tended to be overzealous—even dangerous—in their promised benefits. Believe it or not, Lysol was first advertised as both a household cleaner *and* a women's hygiene product. Hard to even imagine! But by the late 1800s, pain-relieving formula advertisements were finally banned for not only being fraudulent but also downright dangerous as well, with ingredients that maimed and killed.

suggested women not only needed but also wanted. By the time women won the vote in 1920, women's magazines were portrayed as "browse books" for the goods and products women were meant to desire—such as toasters, washing machines, irons, and vacuum cleaners—as well as a showplace for articles on how to use those products and what those products could do for women. For example, an article on effective homemaking and time-saving tips might run alongside a Hoover Vacuum Cleaner ad. Eventually, magazines—in a quasi-partnership with advertisers—provided complimentary editorial content and special considerations on layout and placements. The Campbell Soup Company, for one, advertised so frequently from the 1910s through the 1950s that the company was able to command a premium position in the magazines. Month after month, soup ads appeared on the right-hand page of pubs like *Ladies' Home Journal, Good Housekeeping,* and *Woman's Home Companion* adjacent to cooking, homecare, recipes, and other kitchen-related content. Unrelated articles and short-story fiction were almost considered "bonus content," added to draw women readers to these magazines.

This link between advertising and editorial became so standard that advertising salespeople even directed magazines on where the ads should be placed. If the magazine failed to adhere to their placement demands, it was common for advertisers to jump ship, taking their ad dollars with them—a risk few magazines could afford to take. In many cases, the stipulations were spelled out, particularly before the 1960s and 1970s. Some magazines stood up to the issue, even tried to stay afloat through nonprofit status, grants, and/or subscriptions, but they either soon folded or suffered chronic financial woes. *Ms.* Magazine was one of the first to call out the insidious relationship. In 1990, then Editor-in-Chief Gloria Steinem wrote a revealing piece titled "Sex, Lies, and

Advertising," in which she revealed the struggle of selling ads for a magazine that promoted a feminine agenda. In a bold move, she also revealed the placement demands commonly made by large corporations of common products. For example, the Dow Corporation stipulated that "Vivid and Spray 'n Wash should be adjacent to children or fashion editorial," and "Windex, Drano, Bufferin, and Clairol ads were to be placed next to a full page of compatible editorial," and The DeBeers Diamond Company prohibited magazines from "placing ads next to hard news or antilove/romance themed editorial."[11]

It's no wonder these demands were so specific. It turns out that these orchestrated moves *do* have impact. A 1987 study by the *Journal of Advertising Research* found that the higher the rating of editorial believability, the higher the rating of the surrounding advertising.[12] And while the practice of "product placement" (subliminally placing ads next to corresponding editorial in hopes of higher sales quotas for the product) is not only highly controversial but also frowned upon, it still exists. A 2005 PQ Media report that tracked product placement in so-called "other media" (aside from movies, television, books, and video games) found that the biggest segment of product placement in consumer magazines was not in small, obscure special interest publications like *Garden and Gun*, but in general interest women's titles, "which contributed the highest share of product placement spending at $35.5 million that year."[13]

During the Association of National Advertisers' 2005 Print Advertising Forum in New York, top editors representing the American Society of Magazine Editors (ASME) "denied that their publications—or any major magazine titles—accepted product placements," and certainly not the paid placements being bantered around by the PQ report. But advertisers and agency executives speaking at that same forum implied the practice was not only employed but pervasive. What's more, a survey of members from the Association of National Advertisers (ANA) that was released at the conference showed magazines were the second most common medium for product placement deals after television.[14] And this despite official "guidelines" established by the magazine industry against it (see below).

American Society of Magazine Editors Guidelines for Advertisers and Publishers 2011

Advertising Adjacencies

a. Editors and publishers should avoid positioning advertisements near editorial pages that discuss or show the same or similar products sold by the advertiser (a rule of thumb used by many magazines is, the reader must turn the page at least twice between related ad and editorial).

b. Editors and publishers should also avoid the following:

i. positioning advertisements for products and services endorsed by or associated with public figures near editorial content concerning those public figures

ii. positioning advertisements for motion pictures, television programs, recordings and similar works near editorial content concerning participants in those works

Unfortunately, the updated ASME guidelines are no more followed today than they were when Ms. Steinem found it impossible to please advertisers for *Ms.* magazine. Now, instead of advertisers overtly dictating to magazines where their ads should be placed, the battle for placement becomes an in-house issue between the magazine's advertising sales department—which is trying to please advertisers and make sales—and the magazine's editorial department, which is trying to maintain the integrity of the magazine's editorial content while balancing the need to keep the ad dollars flowing so that they can remain in business. And though readers aren't privy to these behind-the-scenes politics and backdoor deals, the eventual compromises are evident when they flip through the latest copy of any chick slick.

Insider Input

"We live in a day and age where advertising spills over to editorial content, and the type of content that readers want. Editors are constantly in a battle to keep advertisers happy, as well as readers. But the line is thin and often crossed. How many times have you opened up a magazine to see advertorial content spill on to editorial content? Sometimes, the reader cannot even distinguish between the two at first glance."
—Stacy Lipson, freelance journalist

Let's skim through a few magazines to see how the relationship between articles and advertising stacks up today, especially when it comes to beauty and body image:

From the November 2011 issue of *Redbook:*

Page 28: "My Almost Fling: What Happens in Vegas Gets Confessed Right Here," a writer's recount of the wildest moments on her girlfriend getaway.

Page 29: Ad for Jergens Overnight Repair, with the tagline, "The difference between tired skin and rejuvenated skin."

Page 54: "Sizzling Style Tips from Diane von Furstenberg."

Page 55: Ad for Suave Professional Line shampoo and conditioner that portrays twin women's heads with shiny slick hair-do's and the tagline, "Can you tell the difference? Top stylists can't."

Pages 61–62: "Wash Your Face Right," an article on proper technique and steps for cleansing.

Page 63: Dove Body Wash ad; copy reads "Discover the difference of Dove nourishment."

Page 66: "Celebeauties," a column including three new celebrity beauty trends, one being the latest in Hollywood manicures.

Page 67: Essie nail polish ad for the shade Cocktail Bling, with the tagline "I like to arm myself with Cocktail Bling."

Page 68: Antiaging section with an article titled "The Truth about DNA and Antiaging Products."

Adjacent Insert: Three-page foldout ad for Garnier Dark Spot Corrector to erase age spots.

Page 69: "My Hands Are Starting to Look Like my Grandmother's," an article with advice offered from a dermatologist, chemist, and manicurist on keeping hands young.

Page 80: "Lazy Women's Fitness" column, including what to eat for a flatter belly.

Page 81: Ad for Special K dark chocolate protein shakes and protein meal bars.

From the May 2011 issue of *Glamour:*

Page 96: "Spring Bags" (one-page feature showcasing flowered designer handbags).

Page 97: Ad for Maybelline Perfect Pastel Eye Shadow in spring colors.

Pages 118–120: "Your Top Swimsuit Questions Answered," an article with many photos of bikini-clad women.

Page 121: Ad for Sally Hansen Wax Warmer Kit, a plug-in waxing system for no-hassle hair removal.

Page 131: "29 New Things to Do with your Hair," a four-page spread on haircare and styles.

Pages: 130, 133, and 135: Ads for Garnier Fructis Sleek and Shine Serum, shampoo, and styling products.

Page: 144: "Seven Gorgeous Eye Ideas," makeup tips for eyes.

Page 143: Ad for Revlon CustomEyes Shadow and Liner.

Page 196: "Can Jake Survive a Dry Spell?" Can *Glamour's* male columnist go a whole month without sex?

Page 197: Ad for KY Intense female arousal gel.

Hmmm. Seems those ASME advertising "guidelines" are not given much credence.

Sure, it seems harmless—even logical—to run ads near content that's relevant to the products being pitched, but the deeper issue here is that women readers are being played in an orchestrated way by magazines, under the guise of consideration for her interests or well-being. But historically, magazines and advertisers have always played off the woman reader, often taking on a paternalistic role about what best reflects her needs, desires, and sensibilities.

ADS OF THE PAST

Back in the fifties, women's magazines purported that an ideal woman should strive for family togetherness, and reader marketing surveys conducted at the time described this happy, successful woman as one who set up a comfortable married home filled with the newest, most efficient appliances and products of the day, a shiny automobile in the driveway, the latest mixers and utensils in the kitchen, a BBQ grill in the backyard, and a garage filled with cutting-edge tools.

Women's glossies took on the role of educating women about all things domestic, including childcare, marriage, cooking, health, and the products they needed to achieve the ideal of a happy nuclear family. The table of contents in magazines like *Redbook, Ladies' Home Journal*, and *Good Housekeeping* read like a primer for finding your inner June Cleaver, with articles on everything from efficient housekeeping to maintaining your appearance for your husband. And the advertisements blatantly reinforced these apron-wrapped standards. One 1954 *Ladies' Home Journal* ad for Jergens Lotion stated, "For Jane, the best use of Jergens Lotion care is the flattery her hands get from her husband. . . . Keep Jergens Lotion and use it regularly after each chore. You can do a housewife's job, but it's nice to have a sweetheart's hands."

Magazine ads pitched everything from Del Monte Fruit Cocktail (serving suggestion: top a canned ham) and Ford cars to Ipana Toothpaste and General Electric dishwashers, plus just about every other must-have household product of the day. Advertising critics contend that these ads encoded the female identity with their role as homemakers and consumers from the very earliest issues.[15]

These magazines also offered advice to women readers about how to keep her marriage working, suggesting it was the woman's job to keep it "alive." Beginning in 1950, *Ladies' Home Journal* ran a marriage advice column called "Making Marriage Work." Regardless of the issue discussed, it was always the woman's fault since it was her job to care for the marriage in the first place. The advice given to women included, "Don't disturb his belongings. Don't open his wallet or read his mail without his approval. Don't read over his shoulder, either."[16]

These magazines also offered advice to women readers about how to keep their mate aroused, how to meet their man at the door with a hot toddy or cup of cocoa, and how to care for themselves enough to attract a man in the first place. Naturally, this fell in with advertisements for toiletries and cosmetics, such as perfume, lipstick, hair dye, and lingerie. And the ads themselves promised happiness, romance, love, and excitement. Take the Revlon Company's

1952 campaign for Fire and Ice, their iconic shade of red lipstick. It led with provocative pseudofeminist ad copy that read: "Do you dance with your shoes off? Do you secretly hope that the next man you meet will be a psychiatrist? Would you streak your hair with platinum without consulting your husband?"[17] These were daring questions of the day. This was the Fire and Ice girl, a bold counterpart to the June Cleaver ideal.

Then there's Clairol, which debuted its hair dye campaign in 1955, when few American women (other than celebrities and the wealthy) colored their hair. To ferry their product to the masses, Clairol conceived the brilliant idea of depicting the women in their ads as the girl next door. Having color-treated hair was no longer limited to actresses and high society mavens—now every woman could look like a movie star. Overnight, these low-key girl-next-door ads inspired with their slogan, "Does she . . . or doesn't she?" Hair coloring became trendy, with the implication that not only would hiding your gray make you appear younger and more desirable, but it was a must if you wanted to keep your man's interest. Case in point: Clairol Loving Care ran the slogan "Hate that gray? Wash it away," with the tagline, "Makes your husband feel younger too, just to look at you!" Or the campaign by Lady Clairol cream and bleach, which brought platinum shades to American women with slogans like "Is it true blondes have more fun?" and "If I've only one life to live, let me live it as a blonde."[18]

Ouch! Talk about unleashing an epidemic of dark-root syndrome that would pervade the next sixty years and beyond! Iconoclastic comparisons were born, like "Mary Ann or Ginger?" and later, "Farah Fawcett or Jaclyn Smith?"

Advertisers were having a field day at the expense—literally—of women. Pandering to narrow stereotypes of female sensibilities fell to a new low when the automotive market launched its "pink" advertising campaign in the 1960s. Ford, GM, and Chrysler all made changes in car styling and details with the woman consumer in mind. These "adjustments" included brighter colors, more luggage space, extra seat positions, lower steering wheels, and easy-to-maneuver door handles that would prevent fingernail polish from chipping.[19] How thoughtful. Many automakers like GM, Ford, and Chrysler also introduced a new car design, the station wagon, for the woman driver who needed extra space to cart kids and groceries around. And remember the wood paneling? That feature was added to make women drivers feel homey and comfortable, like they were relaxing in their wood-paneled living rooms.

Then there were the automakers who took the "pinking" of their cars too literally, with ad campaigns that followed suit. The 1954–55 Dodge La Femme was Detroit's epitome of femininity, with two-toned paint jobs in color combinations heather-rose and sapphire, or the lavender and white option. The car also featured a matching rose-colored leather shoulder bag, seat upholstery with tiny embroidered rosebuds on it, and a coordinating umbrella. It was marketed to the wives of doctors and bank managers in an era when families had only one car, with the tagline, "Never a car more distinctly feminine than La Femme, the first car created exclusively for women."[20]

Detroit didn't stop there. Later developments in marketing to women included fabric slipcovers that could be changed with the season in varying fabrics and colors—just like for your sofa back home. Women could now "decorate" their cars as if this feminine touch would lure women buyers to the car lot. Luggage to match the interior was another "soft" touch. In 1959, General Motors launched its new Cadillac in powder blue, white, and of course, pink. Unfortunately, their condescending ad campaign put a mother and daughter in complementary outfits next to the car, with a tagline that touted, "One of the special delights which ladies find in Cadillac ownership is the pleasure of being a passenger."[21]

Ouch, GM. Maybe they didn't think women could actually drive the vehicle.

FEMINISM'S INFLUENCE ON ADVERTISING

By the early 1970s, there seemed to be a fifteen-year gap from what appeared in ads to what was going on in real life.[22] Ads that used terms like the "weaker sex" or "little women" offended feminists (and frankly, any forward-thinking woman) who rebuffed the idea of getting married, starting families, and devoting themselves to homemaking—exclusive of pursuing an education and a career path. Ads that portrayed women as subordinate to men began to infuriate the "Mary Tyler Moore" and "That Girl" audience of the day. Feminists began to protest these ads as contemptuous for stereotyping women, portraying them as sex objects, and co-opting the language of the women's movement while hawking an underlying message that women were secondary to men.

One of the first organized protests was in 1969 in front of New York City's Macy's department store. It was in response to a Mattel ad in *Life* magazine that pitched its toy products using the following ad copy: "Little girls dream about being a ballerina or a young fashion model, while boys were born to build, learn, and find science fun."[23] Protesters claimed the ad implied mind-enriching toys were only suitable for boys, not girls. And damn, if the protesters weren't right! Women were simply not going to take it anymore. Sit-ins and confrontations over sexist ad campaigns erupted at *Ladies' Home Journal, Playboy,* and Columbia Broadcasting System

(CBS) on ads ranging from National Airlines "Fly me" campaign, Clairol's "Does she . . . or doesn't she?" and Geritol and Folgers for ads that blatantly devalued women. Feminists later began placing THIS AD INSULTS WOMEN stickers on billboards and posters.

A defining shift in advertising arrived via a 1973 perfume campaign for Charlie perfume by Revlon. The revolutionary ads displayed a pantsuited young woman engaging in traditional outside-the-home activities like walking the city streets or visiting a museum. That same year, Clairol ditched the "Does she . . . or doesn't she" hair-dyeing tagline and portrayed women as artists, doctors, and politicians, with the feminist-slanted tagline, "To know you're the best." L'Oreal later hit the ground running with "Because I'm worth it."

This type of advertising produced a number of successful brands, and sales soared noticeably among the companies using classy prowomen catchphrases and jingles that became so popular, many earwormed their way into pop culture. In the late 1970s, ads for Jean Naté fragrance featured a female jockey and the tagline "Take charge of your life." While Enjoli's famous jingle of the same period, "I can bring home the bacon, fry it up in a pan, and never let you forget you're a man," purported to take advertising to and for women by the balls, but nonetheless played to old stereotypes of gender roles. (Sure, it's okay for women to be successful and capable, as long as she knows who really wears the pants in the relationship.)

By the mid-1980s, the message of female empowerment became the standard marketing ploy in hundreds of ad campaigns, something unimaginable just decades before. Not only had dozens of women entered the advertising field and begun their rise to top positions in the industry, but feminism was here to stay and feminists were uncompromising in calling out manufacturers and advertisers when their ads degraded women. By 2005, women would account for over half those employed in advertising and related fields (52.2 percent), and incredibly, the women who had criticized advertising the loudest beginning in the 1970s were now at the helm of ad campaigns.[23]

A DeBeers diamond ring campaign that proclaimed "Women of the world raise your right hand" encouraged women of marrying age to view diamond rings in a new light. No more were diamonds the province of the right-handed ring finger. Instead, the ads encouraged women to buy them as a statement of their independence and success. One ad's copy touted, "Your left hand says we. Your right hand says me." The promotion of this "me" ring was a declaration of freedom for American women who had not held this level of autonomy before. Suddenly, women with an education, career, and income to spare, married or single, gay or straight, liberal or conservative, were encouraged (albeit via a diamond company) to step up and treat themselves to an expensive bauble they could proudly parade on their right hand. "Because they can." Sales of right-handed diamond rings soared 10 percent following the campaign, which also included tags such as, "Your left hand declares your commitment. Your right hand is a declaration of independence."

Even esoteric products like credit cards jumped into the game when American Express created the "'80s Interesting Lives" campaign, which strove to position the company's ubiquitous square of plastic as the "it" credit card for young career women and men who lived dynamic and multifaceted lives. The ads showed yuppies, the term of the day, living spontaneously via the two-by-three-inch card, stuffing a large piece of expensive art they just purchased into the back of a convertible, or jumping aboard a plane for an unplanned trip to the Australian outback. Suddenly, women were at the helm of the credit decision: to buy or not to buy, and they held the power. The campaign was beyond successful, doubling the amount of women applying for the American Express card. By 1984, 27 percent of American women carried the blue card compared to 10 percent just a few years prior.[24]

But the flipside of these ad campaigns, which were—by advertising standards—strongly feminist, was the creation of the superwoman complex. Suddenly, suit-wearing, briefcase-carrying, confident women who worked outside the home and raised well-mannered children, kept a spotless kitchen, and pleased their man every night was the norm. If we women weren't keeping up with career, kids, cooking, and pleasing our husbands, well, we must be slackers, these campaigns inferred. And it didn't help that editorial content in women's magazines reflected these new ultra-achieving standards as well. Stories like *Cosmo's* December 1980 piece "You're Never too Young to Fib About Your Age. It Can Add

Years to Your Life!" or *McCall's* March 1985 "I'm No Good with Money: A 3-Step Plan to Change All That," as well as *Family Circle's* April 1988 article "How to Clean Your Whole House in Only Two Hours," birthed the be-all mentality that would torment women for decades to come.

Women were being challenged to go big or go home, as the saying goes, and this didn't even take into account the ongoing messaging in both ads and magazine content that we had to be beautiful and fit as well as hyperachieving. Who the hell had time to touch up their roots, let alone get to the gym, when we were expected to juggle so much? But while today's ads have backed off this messaging significantly, we're still faced with the ever-present pressure to do whatever it is we do—career woman, stay-at-home mom, or independent spirit—looking beautiful, ageless, and thin, much like the women who grace the covers of these magazines.

Readers Respond

"It wasn't until I had my first child that I realized how impossible the 'superwoman' standard was. Before, I would see these ads and articles and think, 'Right on, I can be a kick-ass mother, be totally present to my children and partner, have a rewarding career, *and* be emotionally fulfilled.' The reality is that 'having it all' comes at a cost. Ultimately, something or someone gets shortchanged, whether it's your kids, your career, your relationships, or your sanity. I felt like I'd been swindled by our culture, especially because the message was at first so empowering."
—Michelle, communications specialist

* * *

So the question looms, should we expect something more from our favorite women's titles today? That depends. Did we plop our hard-earned dollars down on a subscription all to be deceived? Or did we place our trust in them by picking up the issue in the first place? Since trust is one of the mainstays of loyal readerships, it's important to be aware of the ugly little underbelly that is the truth in advertising: that what you see is not always what you get when you read the women's magazines. Women hold 86 percent of the purchasing power today, a far leap from back in the day when advertisers barely recognized us as consumers. Your voice counts. Don't waste it.

Just knowing there is a fine line between misleading and blatantly false advertising in the magazines may help us be more discerning consumers, since magazines are savvy about making sure they don't cross it. But where do *you* draw the line as the reader? Perhaps you'll draw it where reasonable women are misled. Ultimately, only you can decide how advertising affects you.

Chapter 4

FASHION FORWARD

You either know fashion or you don't.
—Anna Wintour

On the surface, fashion magazines like *Vogue, Harper's Bazaar,* and *Elle* seem like glossy vehicles for designer advertisements and creative fashion spreads and features, but there's much more than meets the eye. Top fashion magazines not only direct fashion trends and make or break a designer's career, they also advocate styles, price points, and beauty ideals that don't always have the reader's best interests in mind, nor those of the models who grace these pages month in and month out.

There's no doubt that fashion photographs have an impact on us. They reflect back to us our desires, fantasies, insecurities, and even our fears. They entertain, arouse, appall, and inspire us—sometimes all at the same time. And that's part of the beauty and disgrace of fashion photography. Eva Mendes splayed out on a chaise longue wearing a silky floral sundress is altogether different than a sexualized ten-year-old girl bedecked in grown-up clothes and heels, her flat chest exposed, her expression sensual (as seen in January 2011 French *Vogue*). Like fashion itself, these photo spreads and advertisements test boundaries and push limits. There are some rules, yes, and every fashion designer and magazine has its unique style, but under all the artifice, creative expression, and pretention, they share one common goal: to market or sell a brand—whether it's the magazine itself, the designer, or both.

Because as it turns out, much like the line between editorial content and advertising, the line between magazine editors and clothing designers is a fuzzy one at best. They depend on each other for survival, and they need you to buy into what they're selling—even if it comes at a deeper cost than a subscription or sales receipt.

How do women's magazines stack up against each other in the fashion game? Let's take a look.

THE FASHION RAG RUNDOWN

Nowadays, most women's magazines include some degree of fashion coverage, but there are several glossies that are true fashion magazines. Tops among them are *Vogue, Elle, W, Harper's Bazaar,* and *Glamour.* However, in the pantheon of true fashion magazines, the most iconic, influential, and widely read is *Vogue,* which has sister editions in sixteen countries, including Spain, France, Italy, and Australia. This century-old veteran and fashionista favorite primarily showcases haute couture, which is handcrafted clothing of the most expensive and luxurious fabrics and detailing, by top designers such as Chanel, Christian Dior, and Jean Paul Gaultier. Rarely does the magazine include clothes with price points below megaexpensive. You won't often see labels from retailers like JCPenney or Kohl's promoted in these pages. This is fashion pretention at its best, but *Vogue* has never pretended to be anything but elite. Unlike more formulaic glossies, like *Glamour* or *Cosmo,* which also toss in fashion spreads, *Vogue* complements its fashion features with more literary content and writing that is smarter, deeper, and less patronizing than what appears in these fluffier counterparts. *Vogue* is also known for its hot celebrity covers and accompanying fashion layouts, which can make or break newsstand sales from one month to the next (see chapter 10 for more on the power of celebrity). The famous September issue, which heralds in the year's fall fashions, can pack six-hundred-plus pages, by far the largest issue of all the fashion magazines. In fact, *Vogue's* September issue is so unrivaled, its production—and Editor-in-Chief Anna Wintour—were the subject of the 2009 documentary titled simply *The September Issue.*

Readers Respond

"I love the artistry of the photography and the beautiful ways they display the clothing. It's also a kick to see what is considered 'in fashion' or what the current trends are. Lately, I've been flashing back to the '70s. What's old is new again."

—Sandi, contract administrator

Next in the harem is *Harper's Bazaar,* which features designer collections from all over the world, including the fashion meccas Milan and Paris. Here you'll find more couture and classic design labels, like Yves Saint Laurent and Dior. *Harper's* strives to set itself apart from other high-end fashion glossies, including *Vogue,* by only including fashion-related editorial content. If it's not about designers, trendy-looking fashions, runway shows, or models, you won't see it in *Harper's*. There are no health or career articles, for instance. Who reads *Harper's*? Affluent, professional women between the ages of thirty-five and fifty-four, with median incomes over $70,000.

Elle, which was launched in 1981 as the American counterpart to the original French version that was created in the forties, is one of the largest fashion magazines in the world. Like *Vogue,* it has sister editions around the world, boasting thirty-six editions on six continents. American *Elle* features high fashion similar to *Harper's* and *Vogue*, but claims it leans toward more affordable, wearable, and accessible clothing—albeit still exclusive, by conventional standards. Here you'll find mostly higher-end labels like Dior, Dolce & Gabbana, and Armani as well as the occasional item you can actually buy at department stores like Macy's. The fashion spreads here, like you'll find in the other magazines, rely heavily on celebrities and thin beauty standards, but they're more playful and less rigid. Unlike the top-tier fashion magazines, *Elle* takes itself less seriously, focusing more on what's trendy and fun in the realm of high-end fashion. As for nonfashion content, it's a middle ground between *Vogue* and *Glamour.* Here you'll find women's issues and lengthy features minus women's magazine staples, like career and money advice.

W magazine, on the other hand, may be the most artistic of the fashion rags, focusing on the true art of fashion, with eclectic, high-end, colorful fashion spreads. *W* splits its heft between fashion spreads and celebrity profiles and spottings, often using celebrities in lieu of models to showcase edgy styles. It concentrates on hip, up-and-coming designers like Tory Burch and Jason Wu, and less on classic designers like Versace or Dior, though their clothing is still showcased as well. Readers are mostly married, educated women with median incomes over the $150,000 mark, indicating they may be both in the market for, and can afford to replicate, a fashion look they see on a celebrity within *W's* pages.

GLOSSY FACT

Vogue's Anna Wintour is given much of the credit for creating the now-standard celebrity fashion spread, where actresses, rather than models, are photographed wearing designer clothes in a fashion layout. She put Kim Basinger on *Vogue*'s cover in May 1991 when actresses were no more model material than the average woman on the street. Winona Ryder and Sharon Stone followed in 1993, Julia Roberts in 1994, and Demi Moore in 1995. Suddenly, it was fashionable to use beautiful actresses to model clothing. Claire Danes, Renée Zellweger, and Sandra Bullock took their turns as *Vogue* cover models later, and the celeb model was born, something done in almost every woman's glossy on the stands today. Usually, the accompanying article includes an exclusive fashion spread featuring the celebrity in a constellation of designer wear.

Glamour, which has become the bridge between higher-end fashion magazines and the Seven Sisters gang, takes a more light-hearted route by including a fashion spread (or three) in between the work, relationship, and health and beauty articles. Fashion features sometimes showcase clothes that young trendsetters could actually wear—perhaps even afford on occasion. Spreads are often colorful, youthful, and playful instead of the more daring, avant-garde or boundary-pushing spreads you'll find in *Vogue* and *Harper's*. Considering its younger demographic (women between the ages of eighteen and forty-nine), this makes sense. Here, advertising also reflects its broader coverage. In addition to ads for Calvin Klein and Tommy Hilfiger, you'll see ads for tampons and yogurt. Thus, *Glamour* is less dependent on designer ads, but it still depends on regular fashion features to win and keep readers.

Similar to *Glamour*, *Marie Claire* includes fashion spreads that are spaced between content on career, health, relationships, women's issues, and politics. The spreads tend to be more eclectic, showcasing a mix of classic and fresh designers in a variety of themed layouts. For example, in the March 2012 issue, they included a modern-day mermaid spread done in soft pinks, blues, and ivories, with the models adorned in feathers, appliqué, lace overlays, and thick-textured wools from the likes of Chanel, Dior, Ralph Lauren, and Calvin Klein. They also list each model's name, the age they were discovered—which is usually a very young twelve or thirteen—their hometown, and playful bits like their guilty pleasure, and the one celebrity they'd like to meet. We aren't offered their current age, but most look no more than sixteen or eighteen.

Other women's magazines, from *InStyle* to *O* magazine, *Self, Shape, Good Housekeeping, Cosmopolitan, Redbook, Essence, Ladies' Home Journal, MORE, Woman's Day* and the rest, give fashion, though perhaps not top billing, a lesser but equally important presence in their pages, showcasing one or more fashion layouts in each issue, complete with theme, story, model type, designer favorites, accessory credits, and their own personal spin on it all.

Why one designer's goods are chosen for a fashion layout while another's are overlooked in any particular magazine during any particular month may be a complex dance that includes the relationship the editors have with each design house, the amount of money the designer lays out in advertising dollars, and a host of other social, personal, and business connections between the two.

A FASHIONABLE AFFAIR

There's a big difference between fashion journalism and fashion advocacy. The latter is what we question here. As it is with advertising in chapter 3, the implication that fashion editors pay homage to designers who have bought their way into the good graces of the magazine by spending mega ad dollars in exchange for coverage of their designs in fashion layouts is the issue. Though we readers may be aware of this symbiotic relationship on the surface, we're not privy to how much the likes of Dior or Calvin Klein are expected to spend in ad money in order for said magazine to grace its pages with their looks in an industry where dozens of other designers are vying for the same editorial space. Furthermore, is that Dior or Calvin Klein design really the trendiest or loveliest fashion since the invention of Velcro, or did those design houses pay the most money for the editors to include it? And if that's the case, can you even trust their fashion opinion?

In 2010, rumors of backroom brokering between designers and editors turned to more than just speculation when the equivalent of a smoking gun was found suggesting that *Harper's Bazaar* very clearly played favorites with big advertisers. According to the fashion blog Racked, a list was left behind on the desktop of a major hotel lobby's public computer that contained the names of designers who were to be used in a ten-page *Harper's Bazaar* editorial fashion shoot.[1] Priority was given in descending order to design houses that had contributed the most ad dollars. Yet below *that* list were the names of designers (listed in alphabetical order) who had not contributed advertising, with instructions that they be worked into the fashion shoot, if possible. The list appeared to be a blatant violation of the Federal Trade Commission's guidelines for advertisers, which states that "advertisers are subject to liability for false or unsubstantiated statements made through endorsements, or for failing to disclose material connections between themselves and their endorsers."[2]

While *Harper's* remained mum, the incident was widely reported by fashion industry folks, who commented that while readers could have guessed that backroom deals took place between fashion mags and designers, this was a rare piece of real anecdotal evidence.

Insider Input

Grace Mirabella, former *Vogue* editor, was once asked where the power in the fashion triangle (designers, buyers, or magazines) lies. She narrowed it down to magazines, saying, "Which is not to say that individual designers don't make important statements. Or that store buyers aren't the first on their block. But finally, finally, the magazines dictate what's at the top. We don't design clothes but we can be very selective in our reporting."[3]

While it's easy to look at the *Harper's* slip-up and wag a finger at the magazine for its blatant favoritism, it's truly sobering when you realize just how serious the fashion game really is.

For instance, in 2011, *Vogue* brought in a staggering $92 million in ad revenue, or 584 pages of ads, for its September issue,

GLOSSY FACT

September is Fall Fashion Month for the glam-rag industry, which means that magazines pull out all the stops with content and fashion spreads, generating hundreds of millions of dollars in advertising revenue.

Here's the rundown of ad pages and revenue generated for September 2011:

Publication	September Ad Pages	1-page Color Ad Rate	Estimated Revenue
Vogue	584	$157,734	$92,116,656
InStyle	431	$151,300	$65,210,300
Elle	350	$141,210	$49,423,500
Harper's Bazaar	308	$105,900	$32,617,200
Glamour	240	$209,954	$50,388,960
W	255	$96,761	$24,674,055
Marie Claire	190	$127,455	$24,216,450
Lucky	189	$119,968	$22,673,952
Cosmopolitan	167	$237,000	$39,579,000

SOURCE: http://adage.com/article/mediaworks/vogue-s-september-issue-leads-fashion-pack-584-ad-pages/228826/

which is the fashion magazine industry's biggest month of the year. And while that's a 10 percent increase over 2010, it's nothing compared to the record-breaking 2007 issue, which included 727 advertising pages—which easily put revenue over the $100 million mark.[4]

But how should we react when magazines are actually *transparent* about favoring advertisers? In the contest to attract ad dollars for the September fashion issue, magazines must get creative. For its 2011 issue, *Glamour* lured in advertisers by offering to include a 2-D bar code for its iPad edition, which readers could photograph and "like" on Facebook. In return, readers would receive special offers from advertisers, fostering potential patronage. *Glamour* called it the "Friends & Fans" app, and advertisers flocked, keeping *Glamour's* ad dollars from suffering a loss over its previous year.

And what of the more subtle influences behind the designers and styles that are advocated in the pages of our glam rags? It's all about relationships, and there's no better name-maker—and breaker—than *Vogue's* own Anna Wintour, who is responsible for some of fashion's heaviest hitters ending up where they are today. In addition to nominating fresh designers for the annual Council of Fashion Designers of America/Vogue Fashion Fund scholarship, she's negotiated many corporate pairings, such as Michael Kors with Sportswear Holdings and Bottega Veneta with Gucci. She helped relaunch down-and-out John Galliano (the first go-around, as he was later suspended from Dior in 2011 after he was caught on video making an anti-Semitic remark to a couple in a French pub), as well as Marc Jacobs at Louis Vuitton.

When asked about the risk of having a bevy of the top designers and houses at her beck and call, many of whom owe her major favors, she insisted she was always open to new design talent but admitted that she liked to stick close to trusty regular designers—

among them Dolce & Gabbana, Marc Jacobs, and Valentino   for each issue's content.[5]

Considering Wintour's legacy, influence, clout, and lengthy family tree of top designers with whom she's connected, it's interesting to note that she's not always been considered the most influential among her contemporaries. Surprise, surprise, Wintour tied for second with *Elle* Editor-in-Chief Robbie Myers, according to a 2008 *Forbes* piece on the most powerful fashion magazine editors in America. Turns out, the top spot went to *Glamour's* Cindi Leive. Of course, *Forbes* used a more fiscally based algorithm to rank the editors, including the monthly unique visitors to each magazine's website, plus their subscription revenue, advertising rates, previous year's ad revenue, and any increases in circulation.[6]

At the time of the ranking, *Glamour* was kicking ass under Leive's reins, with the highest-ever circulation and a huge increase in web traffic. But readers were taken into consideration too, and *Glamour* just may be a more accessible, down-to-earth example of what readers look for in a fashion rag.

"*Vogue's* audience is aspirational, while *Glamour's* audience wants to see products that are in their reach," said Harriet Brown, an assistant professor of magazine journalism at the S.I. Newhouse School of Public Communications at Syracuse University.[7]

*   *   *

In another example of the incestuous relationship between designers and magazines, the high-end clothing-design house Prada invited magazine editors to window-dress and style four different flagship Prada stores around the globe. An editor from *W* styled the New York City SoHo Prada store, the stores in London and Milan were tackled by editors from fashion mags in the United

Kingdom, and Prada in Paris was dressed by Anna Wintour's Parisian counterpart at French *Vogue*.

The editors chose the clothes and arranged and accessorized the mannequins, bringing their vision to the window of the designer's spring collection that year. But should they have? This is just another example that erases any pretense that editors and fashion designers scratch each other's couture-covered backs.

Sometimes, the crossover is literal, further muddying the boundaries. For instance, magazine editors sometime switch sides and become designers, taking with them clout and connections, which they use to finagle their clothing into a magazine's pages. Vera Wang is probably the most notable example, having worked as a fashion editor at *Vogue* for more than fifteen years before becoming a designer. Many editors on the mastheads of magazines also have simultaneously worked as stylists for top designers. While this may make sense, since it's their area of expertise, it comes with questionable ethical dilemmas.

And in yet one more example of this blurry line, in 2011 magazines began selling designer goods straight from their pages. In what's been dubbed a team-up with e-commerce sites, magazines like *Vogue, Harper's,* and *Allure (Esquire* and *GQ* are participating, too) send readers straight to an online service where they can scoop up the very designs showcased in their magazines each month.[8] Magazines get either a fee or a small portion of the sales for sending a certain amount of customers to the e-commerce site. In an effort to become e-tailers, magazines are competing directly with stores like Saks and Neiman Marcus, selling designs by Lanvin, Dior, Marc Jacobs, Stella McCartney, and the rest.

Though women's magazines may never have pretended to be objective observers of the fashion world, they certainly celebrate the most talented designers, laud the up-and-comers with pages of new fashions, and showcase beautiful clothing each month. But are they beautiful clothes because the magazines tell us so, or because the designer is in the editor's proverbial pocket?

The implication is clear: designers are paying for their designs to be showcased in magazines by purchasing advertising, and editors may only be showing those designer's fashions because they were paid to. While on the surface, women may understand that fashion editorial spreads are endorsements, the connections between editors and designers are clearly not disclosed to the readers. Further, there is no fine print at the end of a fashion layout informing us that Tommy Hilfiger or Kate Spade bought three pages of advertising in *InStyle* this month worth $453,900 but it's quietly implied when we see their ads regularly appear in the magazine. And while we're talking figures, let's have a peek into the price points of just what the actual clothes run us in terms of real numbers.

THE HIGH COST OF FASHION, LITERALLY

Even if you love fashion and live for the September issues, women's magazines showcase a slew of clothing, shoes, and accessories that are seriously pricey. These overpriced clothing and accessories are what most women have come to expect from the glossies. Due to the advertiser's influence and the relationships developed between designers and fashion editors, Prada bags and Gucci shoes, Tiffany jewels, Dior dresses, and Versace coats are standard fare. Occasionally, magazines like *Glamour* and *Cosmo* and a few others throw women a bone by including items from retailers like Anthropologie, H&M, Banana Republic, and other semiaffordable retailers, again usually based on their advertising pool. This must-have loot the mags run month in and month out is promoted in an almost advertorial setting that screams, "You must have this dress!" or "This is the 'it' bag this season." Often, readers have to look closely to distinguish between a page of advertising and a page of editorial since they are both clearly selling the design goods on each page. One caveat is that some fashion magazines like to promote accessories and fashions that are "good deals." Those items are often couched in buy-for-less articles, which compare a high-end designer fashion, like a $700 dress from Diane von Furstenberg, with a $70 retail chain look-alike from Banana Republic. In the March 2012 *Glamour,* cover girl Amanda Seyfried's look is replicated with earrings from jewelrybox.com, jeans from American Eagle, and shoes from the Jessica Simpson collection, coming in at likely a twelfth of the price of the clothing she wears on the cover. Likewise, the January 2012 *Cosmo* replicates the look of stars' expensive outfits with reasonable chain-store knockoffs.

The message being sold is that these high-price-point items are fashionable, and if you're the trendy type, you really should be buying into them, literally. If you can't, well, the next best thing is the cheap page of deals and steals, replications and reproductions, which some of the magazines do include each month. Of course, the inference here is that if you don't spring for the pricey goods, you're just not as cool. Unfortunately, the average magazine reader can't afford to dress-out their closets with much of the pricey clothing, jewelry, shoes, and accessories that are advertised, which only enhances their desirability. And most real women don't live the requisite lifestyles in which to wear these fashions. In fact, the median income range for *Glamour* readers is $63,500, while *Lucky* boasts a reader average income of $82,000, and *Vogue's* is $63,094. But expensive brands, and the status they confer, have long been alluring to women, young and old.

A 2009 study in the *Journal of Brand Management* found that "fashion brands are seen as strong vehicles for expressing self-concept. . . . They help to achieve an image and signify a group membership mentality."[9] Study author Angela Carroll says there's an implied social code with the coveted brands, as well as a negative connotation that comes with unbranded fashion goods, whereby "belongers" need the branded fashion merchandise to affirm their social identity. Basically, this means the hippest fashion brands make you feel cooler and help you conform to your peers, especially for the young consumer.

Case in point: how often do you see ads, fashion spreads, and celebrity profiles of women bedecked in clothes from Target, which sells quality brands at affordable prices?

However, some designers are attempting to bring their fashions to the masses. Karl Lagerfeld, Stella McCartney, Versace, and

Readers Respond

"One of my gripes is the 'How to Get This Outfit for Less' features, where the cheaper version is only $500. Who spends that much? Nobody I know. If magazines really wanted our attention, they would create a look appropriate for dropping your kids off at school, going into the gym to exercise, and then going to the grocery store—all without changing. I actually remember an article about ten years ago where Josie Bissett [of the show *Melrose Place*] did a layout of what new moms should wear. I headed straight to Old Navy with my magazine and copied her looks."

—Ann, court reporter

Marni all designed collections for H&M, which is the proverbial bridge between Target and Macy's. Jason Wu, Missoni, and Zac Posen designed for Target, and Vera Wang for Kohl's. These are midlevel retail prices with a designer label attached. And they've been wildly successful: Jason Wu's fifty-three-piece collection for Target reportedly sold out both online and in stores the same day it launched, according to *US Weekly*.[10] Likewise, Missoni sold out its four-hundred-piece designer collection for Target overnight at most stores, and customers crashed the website several times on launch day in the madness to scoop up designer labels.[11]

Like fine art, or a well-engineered car, high-end clothes have a place and a target market. And while we can't all afford these luxuries, we certainly can admire and fantasize about them, which is one of the biggest allures of fashion magazines. Being transported out of the conventional, appreciating the artistry, or flinching at

GLOSSY FACT

According to a 2011 *Wall Street Journal* article titled "How Can Jeans Cost $300?" the markup of designer clothing is 2.2 to 2.6 times cost.[12] That means a designer dress that cost $500 to create will cost $1,300 (500 x 2.6) by the time it reaches a swanky store. The magic compounding the price also includes the designer's current cache and popularity, how high-end the store is, and the region in which it's located. New York or Los Angeles obviously command higher prices than a city in Middle America.

the vulgarity of fashions has long been a favorite pastime, whether we can afford to buy into them or not.

THE (YOUNG) FACES OF FASHION

Of course the price isn't the only problem plaguing the fashion industry. What about the women modeling the merchandise? For starters, we must use the word "women" loosely since the average age of models has slipped precariously below the standard once considered the norm, and with that brings a host of accompanying labor laws and moral and ethical dilemmas that come with using young, underage girls to model adult clothing.

Also asking those questions is The Model Alliance, a new nonprofit group dedicated to improving working conditions in the American modeling industry. At the start of the February 2012 Fashion Week, Alliance founder and model Sara Ziff delivered an impressive speech that raised concerns about the crisis of eating disorders and body image issues among models, challenging the industry to not only rethink size standards, but also improve financial transparency and bolster and enforce child labor laws. Ziff laid out additional goals for the Alliance, including instituting a backstage privacy policy at fashion shows and a system to anonymously counsel models on workplace abuse, among other recommendations. She also presented a draft of a models' bill of rights. Coco Rocha, the Canadian model who's been an outspoken advocate against eating disorders in the industry, cohosted the evening, remarking, "This is about our rights as human beings, as women and men."[13]

Ziff, who filmed the 2010 semiautobiographical documentary *Picture Me* about the abuses in the modeling industry, emphasized numerous issues as the foundation of the Alliance's mission, recalling when she'd been put on the spot to take age-inappropriate photos. She also spoke of feeling that agencies have in the past been dishonest in their bookkeeping practices at the expense of models. There was plenty of support from models in the industry, asserting that they need some sort of representation and protection, especially underage girls, since modeling without any kind of mentor or chaperone is a recipe for abuse and manipulation.

In *Picture Me,* Ziff exposes the compromising positions in which young models may find themselves. Teenage girls are asked to dress down to nearly nothing or even to get naked during a photo shoot. One young model in the documentary shares how she took off her clothes with no problem, but when the photographer took his off, too, she started to understand the creepy and inappropriate implication. Another model recounts how a photographer asked her to come to the hot tub after a shoot, and she just assumed everyone from the photo shoot would be there, so she agreed. But when she arrived, she discov-

Insider Input

"More than ever, the media is enforcing overt sexual behavior on young girls. I know when I was modeling, my agent told me at sixteen that she wanted me to take 'sexier' pictures, and many of the photographers were pushing me to wear something sheer, with small shorts, and tossing around the word 'sexy' before I was eighteen. With fans blowing my hair, a top that showed my midriff, and tight jeans—it took a toll on my self-image from a young age."

—Nicole Weider, former Victoria's Secret model

ered that he was the only one in the hot tub—naked, to boot. Feeling uncertain about what to do, she said she got in (wearing her bathing suit), and he immediately tried to grope her breasts. When she shunned his advances and got out of the tub, clearly miffed, he said, "Oh, aren't we on the same page?" To which she replied, "You're forty-five, I'm sixteen; no we're not on the same page."[14]

A fourteen-year-old is barely learning how to assert herself as an individual, let alone when she's in a situation like that. And how easily can she stand up for her rights and, say, refuse to walk a runway with her ass half exposed if a big-name designer's stylist is insisting that she does? Her career is at stake and she may not have the wisdom or courage to just say no. She shouldn't have to in the first place.

Another hot-button issue among models and their advocates is remuneration for walking in a fashion show. Apparently, while top models earn megabucks, and lesser models earn some level of pay, it's just as likely that young, unknown models are "paid" in the way of clothes from a designer's collection, or they simply work in exchange for "exposure" on the catwalk—in more ways than one. And if a model isn't happy with that, or complains about the conditions, there are ten other young wannabes itching to nab her spot in a show or photo shoot.

The pressure to start modeling younger and younger in an industry where you're all but dried up by your early twenties is all-consuming. Models as young as thirteen and fourteen are widely sought, especially those from small-town Middle America and impoverished Eastern European cities who are more likely to be exploited and objectified without chaperones to look out for their welfare.[15]

Worse, adult models with almost-real-looking bodies can't even compete next to these adolescent and sometimes prepubescent girls in their own industry. How does this serve adult women who are reading fashion magazines?

Under scrutiny recently has been the fact that girls as young as ten are modeling, posing in seductive, sexualized clothing

and full makeup and stilettos. In a January 2011 French *Vogue*, ten-year-old Thylane Blondeau is sprawled seductively on tiger-print bedding wearing very grown-up looking diamond jewelry and full makeup, with her waist-length locks swept into a sophisticated up-do. In another, she wears a gold lamé dress that is cut to the waist, with matching gold stilettos (though of course, her flat chest peaks from beneath the fabric, as she has no cleavage, let alone breasts). Critics blasted both the magazine's fifteen-page spread, guest edited by designer Tom Ford, as well as the child's modeling agency and parents for the debacle. Parents groups issued statements of condemnation, and bloggers worldwide called the whole thing creepy, in the same way kiddie pageants are offensive.

Of course, sexualizing young girls in the interest of fashion is not a new trend. Remember Brooke Shields and Calvin Klein, and the famous tagline: "Nothing gets between me and my Calvins"?

The ads were overtly sexual, and Brooke? She was barely fifteen. This began an era of blatant sexual ads starring half-clad young teen girls, which continued to escalate in raunch factor until the public, religious organizations, and citizen groups began to call for boycotts. Apparently, not much has changed—except that the girls keep getting younger.

Another ten-year-old to hit the big labels is Cindy Crawford's own daughter, Kaia, who is the newest face of Versace. Her entrance into the modeling world sparked worldwide debate. Op-eds, blog posts, and websites buzzed with the news of the mini Crawford model, and the "how young is too young" argument. In the midst of that storm, Mom put the brakes on, telling *Fashion Week Daily*, "At this point, she's too young to pursue a career. There's not even a handful of jobs for a ten-year-old girl. But if she's seventeen and wants to try it, of course, what can I say?"[17]

But we're left wondering if Crawford pulled the plug because there truly are no jobs for prepubescent models, or because the chatter surrounding a ten-year-old as the face of a designer campaign was too controversial.

Likewise, Kate Moss's thirteen-year-old sister, Lottie, has also entered the fray. In her test photos, which hit the Internet in 2011, she appeared sultry and grown up, with tousled hair, heels, and shorts, and come-hither expressions—looking well beyond her thirteen years.

Fourteen-year-old Hailee Steinfeld, a child actress, became the face of Miu Miu's fall 2011 campaign. And Hailee isn't the only young starlet courted by the fashion houses. Thirteen-year-old Elle Fanning followed her big sister, Dakota, into the branding arena when she became the face of Marc Jacobs 2011 fall campaign, looking quite grown up in a full-length fur coat, wide-legged wool pants, and a cropped blouse.

Then there's Dakota herself, who posed quite suggestively in an ad for Marc Jacobs' Oh, Lola perfume, which is named for the sexually precocious twelve-year-old character in Vladimir Nabokov's infamous 1955 novel *Lolita*. Jacobs caught flak from the British Advertising Standards Authority (BASA) when it banned the ad, which shows Dakota sitting on the floor, leaning back on one thin arm, looking languid, wearing a pale lace polka-dotted dress, and squeezing a giant pink bottle of perfume between her outstretched legs. To say it looked phallic is an understatement. And that was the purpose! More concerning, however, is that the shot intentionally makes Fanning out to look childlike rather than grown up. As Jacobs told *Women's Wear Daily,* "When we were speaking about who to use in the Oh, Lola fragrance ads, I had recently seen *The Runaways*. Dakota was in it, and I knew she could be this contemporary Lolita, seductive yet sweet."[18]

The BASA, none too pleased by the overt sexuality of the ad, stated: "We understood the model was seventeen years old, but we considered she looked under the age of sixteen. The length of her dress, her leg, and position of the perfume bottle drew attention to her sexuality. Because of that, along with her appearance, we considered the ad could be seen to sexualize a child."[19]

Again, it reeks of creepy child porn, which is apparently the hot look in fashion. Of course, the artistic eye is subjective, and photographers, designers, and others in the industry who are caught in the crossfire often defend it as "art" and "freedom of expression." True enough, but when most of the public's interpretation skews towards kiddie porn, there's a problem.

Meanwhile, child labor laws, pay equality, and the fight against sexism, objectification, and harassment for young models who estimates say average a modest $27,000 annually and are encouraged to drop out of school and work for a piece of possibly

"'Truth in advertising' should include information on the age of the models in all women's magazine photos, whether it's in ads or content. These are girls—not just teenagers—but sometimes girls as young as ten, eleven, and twelve, in the case of some fashion ads. They sell them to us as the image of the ideal woman. Throw in the added insult of photo retouching, and you end up with an absurd body image that no real adult woman can match."
—Roxanne Hawn, magazine writer

unwearable couture, are important topics being addressed by the Model Alliance. The Council of Fashion Designers in America (CFDA) and *Vogue* magazine have already offered to support changes within the industry. Prime among the issues are that young models have become easy prey for the industry to take advantage of on many levels.

In *Picture Me,* Ziff also exposes how models are exploited financially. For instance, when new models are signed with agencies, it's standard practice for them to be flown to their destination countries, provided a car and driver, an apartment, and copies of their portfolio book, which is sent around to fashion houses—all at their own expense, as the agency bills them for each of these items. Girls can rack up quite a debt, and these costs are subtracted from their earnings—when they finally have them. But the more runway shows the models are cast for, the more exposure they get. And the bigger the show, the better the odds that a prominent fashion magazine editor may see and request them for future editorial work, which leads to the best money in the business. Just

GLOSSY FACT

The Model Alliance surveyed eighty-five fashion models currently working in the industry in 2012, with an average age of twenty-six. These were some of the results:

- 76.5 percent have been exposed to drugs or alcohol on the job.
- 64.1 percent have been asked to lose weight by their agencies.
- 29.7 percent of models have been touched inappropriately on the job.
- 28 percent have been pressured to have sex with someone on the job.
- Of those who've experienced sexual harassment, only 29.1 percent felt they could tell their agencies.
- 86.8 percent have been asked to pose nude.

source: http://modelalliance.org/industry-analysis

as editors like Anna Wintour can make or break a designer, so it is with the models themselves.

No matter what her age, if a model is liked, she's golden; pass her over enough and she goes home broke.

THE UGLY SIDE OF THE BEAUTY IDEAL

And contrary to how you might believe models are treated like golden girls, the reality of the industry shows they're nothing more than livestock—prodded in and examined for flaws. In Ziff's documentary, many young girls attest to being treated simply as a body, describing scenes in which stylists talk about the models as if they're not right there in front of them. "We'd put her in that outfit, but her ass is too big, her thighs too fleshy," recalls one model in the documentary. Yet clearly, no size 2 has an ass that's too big or thighs that are truly fleshy. These girls are simply the illusion of the fashion industry, in which clothes supposedly look better on an uberthin hanger. And models are not above degradation from all sides of the equation.

Insider Input

"I had a problem with the way we were treated, not only on the set, but also at go-sees. Think Simon [Cowell] on steroids, and that's pretty much how they talked to us. 'Hmm . . . thighs are too muscular. Not enough space between them. Cankles. Head's too big. Head's too small. Too black—all anyone will see are eye-whites and teeth. Paste-*y*. Your skin is almost see-through!' I've heard it all. We were treated like cattle and talked to like idiots."
—Diane Faulkner, former model

Upon the unveiling of the 2012 *Sports Illustrated* swimsuit cover, Sophia Neophitou, the woman who casts the annual Victoria's Secret Fashion Show, said she'd never deign to let the *Sports Illustrated* cover girl, Kate Upton, walk that coveted runway. She told *The New York Times* that "we would never use Upton because her look is 'too obvious' to be featured in the high-profile production." She then called Upton a "page 3 girl," referencing the busty, barely clad women featured in *The Sun*, a London tabloid. "She's like a footballer's wife, with the too-blonde hair and that kind of face that anyone with enough money can go out and buy."[20]

Really? What's the point of degrading the twenty-two-year-old model who had just made the sought-after cover of the ubiquitous *Sports Illustrated* with such hostile comments? Talk about an undermining, backbiting industry.

Then there's the ubiquitous issue of eating disorders. We've already seen a grassroots movement in the industry with regard to eating disorders. Many models have opened up about having, if not the clinical definitions of anorexia or bulimia, disordered and extremely unhealthy eating habits. Why wouldn't they? Models are almost expected to abstain from solid food the day before a shoot or fashion show so their tummy won't bulge, and they often follow ritualistic and even dangerous diet plans several weeks before big modeling events. These young girls and women don't always effortlessly keep their weight down, after all. The desired hip circumference in the industry is thirty-four to thirty-five inches, with an anything-over-and-you're-out mentality. How do they

Insider Input

"I remember one of the models who was with my agency told me she frequently swallowed cotton balls of orange juice to 'fill her up' with the orange flavor."
—Nicole Weider, former Victoria's Secret model

GLOSSY FACT

In a 2006 study published in the *Journal of Human Sciences* on how models were portrayed across four different women's magazines—*Fitness, InStyle, Good Housekeeping*, and *Glamour*—researchers found that thin women were more frequently portrayed in *Fitness* magazine and that average-size women appeared most frequently in *Good Housekeeping*. The study looked at forty ads that ran in the four magazines between the years 2003 and 2005. Models portrayed in the most respectful body positions were most frequently (and predictably) found in *GH*, while women who were photographed in submissive/sexual body poses were seen mostly in *Glamour. Glamour* also ran the highest frequency of women who were nude or scantily dressed. The thinnest models were portrayed in *Fitness* and *InStyle.*[21]

The study is important because it showed that magazines geared toward younger women objectify women as primarily sexual beings, thus sending the message that this is an ideal body type and aesthetic to model.

measure up, literally? Statistics show that most models are be-tween the ages of fourteen and nineteen, with an average height of between five ten and five eleven, and an average weight between 120 and 124 pounds. The healthy weight for a woman who is five feet ten is between 142 and 150 pounds, with models weighing 23 percent less than the average woman.[22]

Go back half a century, and the average model in the 1960s was about five foot seven and weighed 129 pounds. And in the 1980s, curvier models like Christie Brinkley and Cindy Crawford were taller and thinner but still possessed a healthy BMI. By the 1990s, however, the emaciated look of "heroin chic" made its way to the runway and to the pages of the glossies, and a troubling trend became more deeply rooted.

In 2007, the Council of Fashion Designers of America (CFDA) created a health initiative to raise awareness of eating disorders in the fashion industry and to try to bring change to the desired look of the models on runways and in magazines from the skeletal look to a more realistic ideal. Unfortunately, the CFDA really only raised the ire of models and critics when they took on a righteous stance, downplaying the role the industry plays in the crisis. In a letter from CFDA president Diane von Furstenberg, the coun-cil seems to place the blame on the models instead. An excerpt from the 2010 letter states: "No single influence is responsible for the development of eating disorders. Genetics, neurochemistry, personality, weight-conscious occupations, and sociocultural fac-tors all play a role in the etiology of these illnesses. Five percent of women in the United States struggle with anorexia nervosa or bulimia nervosa at some point in their lives."[23]

Here is the very industry blaming personality and genetics rather than holding themselves up to scrutiny. Not a very fashion-able move.

"There were several things we were encouraged to do to be camera-ready. The favorite was to nibble on chocolate Ex-Lax and drink close to a gallon of room-temperature water a day. No salt of any kind. No pop. No caffeine. This is all done three days before a shoot. The idea was that this regimen would keep our stomachs flat and keep us from bloating."

—Diane Faulkner, former model

What do you want to guess is the percentage of models who struggle with an eating disorder? Well, one 2008 Italian study found that 54.5 percent of fashion models had a BMI under eighteen, which indicates probable eating disorders, and 5 percent were diagnosed with a clinical eating disorder much younger than nonmodels of the same age.[24]

The fact is, models wouldn't be dying to achieve thinness if designers and industry insiders made good on their promise to use meatier women with curves and those over the age of sixteen, as the council suggested. The guidelines presented by the council include encouraging models to receive regular medical care and advising those who may have an eating disorder to seek professional help in order to continue modeling. *Hmmm . . .* a preventive guideline might be a little more successful and more on point, no?

Or how about forcing designer hands to create larger sample sizes of the designer's clothing that models must fit into; say, no less than a size 4 as opposed to the size 0 to 2 that models are literally dying to fit into. The premise of the guidelines is that models must do a better job of managing the stress of being unrealistically thin. Yes, that sounds like the solution to this insidious issue, right? Not so much.

An editorial on the CFDA site cowritten by Furstenberg, who's also a veteran fashion designer, acknowledges that there's a lot of pressure from the industry to be thin, but it still places most of the blame on models. "Some models have difficulty maintaining the body ideal as they move into adulthood," it reads, "and run the risk of engaging in unhealthy eating behaviors that lead to eating disorders."[25]

Well, what exactly would you have them do to fit into the too-thin ideal, Ms. von Furstenberg? Oh yeah, see the doctor more often and get help with their eating disorder when they hit a mammoth brick wall or a complete collapse of their health. Shit, that's brilliant.

Readers Respond

"A few years back, the nine-year-old girl I was babysitting held up the cover of *Seventeen* and went, 'I'm fat. Look at her, she's pretty.' And then she pointed to a picture of a model in *Seventeen,* and said, 'But *she's* not fat.' I looked at the picture, and the model was maybe a size 2. It was sad."
—Stacy, writer

Instead, the industry blames bad genes and personality issues for predisposing models to eating disorders. And worse, it leaves the models at the heart of fixing the whole problem themselves. When in fact, the council could foster real change by instituting guidelines wherein designers couldn't hire women under certain weights, under certain measurements, and under certain ages. Why not mandate sample clothes as size 4 or 6, or require that half a designer's show must consist of women over a certain age or weight? No, that would take the blame off the models and put it back on the industry, wouldn't it?

The guidelines also call upon designers to support the well-being of younger models by not hiring those under the age of sixteen for runway shows and not letting those under eighteen work past midnight. The fashion industry and the academic eating disorders community participated in a CFDA-hosted panel discussion titled "The Beauty of Health: Resizing the Sample Size" in 2010. Designers, magazine editors, and casting directors in attendance spoke of the need to improve model's lives and encourage healthy lifestyles, but no one's seemed to manage to resize a thing in the interim.

And sadly, this pervasive belief that thin is the beauty ideal informs even how women outside the fashion industry are judged.

Insider Input

"Although the modeling industry has slowly embraced more curves, on the runway it is still impossibly stick-skinny, with the models showing their ribs and shoulder bones. They feel the pressure to stay this skinny because the designers want to make sure they are 'clothes hangers' and not get their body in the way of the clothing. It is truly tragic."

—Nicole Weider, former Victoria's Secret model

Take designer Karl Lagerfeld's comment to the *Metro*, a European daily newspaper: "The thing at the moment is Adele. She is a little too fat, but she has a beautiful face and a divine voice."[26] He later backtracked and recanted the comment, saying it was taken out of context and not at all the way it was intended. Lagerfeld even shared that he lost a whopping thirty kilos over a decade ago and he knows how hard it can be to struggle with weight. Again, he put his foot in his mouth, since his comments implied that Adele is "struggling" in any way with her size. Writers at the website Jezebel poked fun by saying, "Internationally recognized weight management expert/robot Karl Lagerfeld is walking back his comments to *Metro* that singer Adele is 'a little too fat.'"[27]

As if that weren't humiliating enough for Adele, *Vogue* also seemed to discriminate against her voluptuousness, only in a less vocal but nonetheless overt way. In March 2012, Adele graced the cover of this titular fashion magazine. Usually, a cover is complemented by a generous fashion spread on the interior. Unfortunately, aside from the cover and one couched shot of the singer in a beautiful black embroidered top and marigold silk taffeta dress by Oscar de la Renta, shot in extremely low lighting complete with strategic manipulation of Adele's figure, there are no other photos other than a headshot in this spread. It seems *Vogue* had a quibble with Adele's ability to be a fashion icon, despite putting her on the cover and giving her the *Vogue* nod of approval. When it comes to thinner actresses and singers, they're usually given the six- to eight-page minimum spread, along with an incredible array of clothing changes, often shot in an exotic photo location, so Adele's half-assed treatment seems a little shameful. In fact, the one shot they do provide is so stunning we'd have preferred another handful.

* * *

Fashion rags and those glossies that include fashion have a responsibility not only to their readers but also to the models who grace their pages. Rather than turn a blind eye to underweight, underage, underrepresented ethnicities or sexually inappropriate fashion photography, editors should actively rectify those issues in their magazines, support mandates and grassroots efforts to end exploitation, and strive to see that the fashion industry and those involved don't sweep horrors under the rug, but hold them up to the light instead. Where once women defined their personal style by the fashions they read about and emulated in the glossies, we now question some of the more insidious messages conveyed via the fashion imagery we see in magazines. Regardless of whether you devour these magazines monthly, hooked by the alluring and the lurid that's reflected in the layouts, or you just skim through them on the way to the heavier-hitting articles, remember that you can voice your concerns about the ugly underside of the fashion industry not only by which brands you choose to wear, but also by which magazines you buy and trust.

Chapter 5

IT AIN'T ABOUT INNER BEAUTY

*Women's magazines punish us with their gorgeous photographs of
Cameron Diaz's ass and snappy diet ideas on the next page.*
—Anna Johnson, author

How do cover lines like "Resize Your Thighs," "Blast Belly Fat,"
and "Take Ten Years Off Your Face" strike you? A tad insulting, perhaps? Most likely. Because the message being sent is that
you, dear reader, are in need of resizing, fat-blasting, and age-de-
fying. And it doesn't stop there. Every month, from every cover,
the magazines scream some new directive that assumes you're not
good enough as you are: "Get Thinner." "Get Prettier." "Exercise
More." "Quit Looking Your Age." "Younger is Better.""Thinner Is
Best." "Put Down that Ding Dong, Dammit!"

Geez, can't a woman get a break already? Not only is this
messaging ridiculous and depressing, it promotes a false beauty
ideal that's largely unattainable for the average woman. Unlike
the models and celebrities gracing these pages, we can't airbrush
off our arm flab, stretchmarks, wrinkles, tummy pooch, or the
cellulite we're genetically predisposed to, and it takes more than a
crash diet and a few sets of donkey kicks to achieve and maintain

the tight ass and flat belly of the fitness model who's showing us these moves.

But hey, keep trying, these magazines tell us. Keep reaching for the holy grail of beauty we're holding out just beyond your grasp, the one that makes you feel fat, frumpy, and forsaken. And since you're clearly having such an impossible time achieving this standard, we're only too happy to *continue* providing you with articles and advertisements that tout (unrealistic) solutions to being less fat, frumpy, and forsaken.

Gee, thanks.

Month after month, chick slicks illustrate how to lose weight, look younger, erase fine lines, whiten teeth, smooth rough skin, buy the best treadmill, and whittle ourselves down to their ideal size 0—no matter what your body type and height.

While the average woman is five foot four inches tall and wears a size 12, the magazines are filled with women who are five eleven and wear a size 2. They all seem to hover in the twentysomething age bracket, and their bodies are as mythic as Greek goddesses, whether sporting bikinis for magazines like *Fitness* and *Shape* or decked out in couture for the covers of *Vogue* and *Elle*. No wonder we feel like schlumpadinks.

According to one study conducted by researchers at the University of Missouri, after just one to three minutes of exposure to the types of images routinely found in women's magazines, young women hate themselves more than they already do.[1]

The female standard, according to the study, is represented by a woman who wears a size 4 in the hips, a size 2 in the waist, and rocks a size-10 bust. The study reiterates that this is "thinner than the average woman and genetically impossible for most women to attain." But are we all really lacking such backbones? Do we feel badly we don't look like the women in the magazines? Apparently, some of us do.

The authors of the study reported that whether a participant was "thin or heavy, confident or prone to self-objectification, the result was the same: the women were equally affected by viewing the images of thin women and showed increased body dissatisfaction after viewing appearance-related images."

The study was made up of eighty-one European American women split into two groups. One looked at ten "neutral" advertisements: ads with images that did not include people. The other group looked at five "neutral" advertisements and five "appearance-related" ads. The ads pictured European American women who were said to "embody cultural ideals of thinness and attractiveness."

No wonder we've become a nation of fad dieters and disordered eaters.

MAGAZINE DIETS DU JOUR

Women's magazines tout a few basic concepts, but diet, aging, and beauty are tops. In particular, these glossies are masters at hammering home weight loss as an issue. Month in and month out they promise to help you shed unwanted pounds, once and for all. Since 45 percent of women are always on a diet, what better way to sell subscriptions? In fact, weight loss is a $40 billion mega industry for which these magazines are largely to thank.[2]

In this month's cover headlines on my coffee table alone, *Woman's Day* shouts, "Real-Life Diet Tricks That Work"; *Self* proclaims, "Yes! You Can Have DIET SUCCESS"; *Ladies' Home Journal* touts, "A Swimsuit That Looks Good on You"; *Women's Health* screams, "Look Great Naked"; and *Redbook* asks, "Ready for a Slimmer, Happier You?"

In article after article, magazines claim if you just master their diet tips and tricks, it's effortless. The problem is, it's not.

Statistics show that the average dieter begins and breaks four diets a year, and that only one in every one hundred people who goes on a diet succeeds in losing weight permanently. The rest gain it back again, often putting on an additional 10 percent more than they shed in the first place.[4] And the magazines seem to know this. Otherwise, how could they sell us a similar cover line the very next month if we had followed their diet and lost the weight just four weeks before? We buy right into their fat, frumpy beauty myth that we won't ever lose weight without *these articles* in *these magazines.*

How does that make us feel? Stressed, discouraged, maybe even a little fatalistic. And surprise, surprise, research shows that stress and depression are primary reasons diets fail. A survey of 17,000 women showed that 99 percent of people who broke their diets did so because they were stressed, depressed, or bored.[5] Essentially, it's the emotional component, not a lack of willpower, that causes diets to fail. Thus, when it comes to magazines, women readers who are concerned about body image (and who isn't, after skimming these glossies?) are caught up in a fairly negative yo-yo dieting loop that keeps them coming back, month after month, in what seems a pretty clear cycle of unhealthy codependence.

GLOSSY FACT

A 2011 *Glamour* magazine survey revealed that 97 percent of women say thirteen negative body thoughts to themselves daily like "I hate my stomach" or "I'm ugly."[6]

Sadly, this obsession costs us. As you learned in chapter 3, advertising and thin ideals are shown to contribute significantly to low self-esteem and body image issues, which are shown to lead to extreme eating disorders, such as anorexia and bulimia. But what of the middle-grounders? The hundreds of thousands— if not millions—of women who, while they haven't fallen into that awful vortex, are nonetheless using some form of disordered eating to address body image issues? You know, the ones always trying to shed those last five to ten pounds.

In an ironic but laudable twist, *Self* magazine—a mainstay of the Pink Ghetto—partnered with the University of North Carolina at Chapel Hill on a 2008 survey of women and dieting. Of the more than 4,000 women who responded, they found 65 percent of American women between the ages of twenty-five and forty-five reported having disordered eating behaviors, and eating habits that women thought were normal—like banishing carbs, skipping meals, and crash dieting—were in fact symptoms of disordered eating.[7]

Although the methods of disordered eating the survey uncovered aren't deadly, like anorexia nervosa or bulimia, women reported that—surprise!—their eating behaviors were the results of emotional and physical stress. Although you might think eating disorders only affect teens and young women, the survey found that women in their thirties and forties suffer from disordered eating at the same alarming rates as young women.

Readers Respond

"I think magazines and ads have somehow decided what is beautiful for us. Now that I'm older, I'm more aware of it and stay away from them as much as I can. The last time I purchased a magazine—about ten years ago—it was for an article titled '10 Easy Ways to Lose Fat.' When one of the 'ways' was to switch from oatmeal, which had 3 grams of fat, to cream of wheat, which had 0 grams of fat, I thought, really, is that what's holding me back?"
—Ann, court reporter

That's an important distinction, since women's magazines seem to approach beauty, body image, and dieting advice as if we were still twenty-five.

The problem is, our body changes significantly as we age. Our metabolism slows down, gravity's relentless pull shifts our flesh southward, muscle tissue is harder to maintain, pregnancy and childbirth leave their own irrevocable marks, and changes in lifestyle and athletic ability slow our caloric burn.

According to Dr. Pamela Peeke, author of *Body for Life,* women begin to lose muscle tissue at an average of about half a pound per year, beginning at age forty. When we lose muscle, our resting metabolism dips, and we burn fewer calories.[8] Thus, unlike younger women, not only do we typically gain weight once we hit forty, we have a much harder time losing it.

You wouldn't know it, looking at the relentless parade of flawless forty- and fifty-something celebrities who appear monthly in magazines without a sag, bulge, or wrinkle to show for their longevity. Talk about the pressure to age gracefully! (More on aging in chapter 6.) Sure, some spend literally hours every day maintaining that perfect shape (think Jennifer Aniston), but what about all the small indignities, like sagging skin, wrinkles, cellulite—all hallmarks of an aging woman—that we *don't* see?

THE ERA OF AIRBRUSHING

When it comes to authenticity about aging and beauty, some magazines have made gestures toward full disclosure. In September 2002, *MORE* magazine published a bold piece on Jamie Lee Curtis, titled "True Thighs." Curtis, who graced the cover in pearls and a slinky black gown, was made up to perfection, then posed for the cover story inside the magazine barefoot, without makeup, wearing nothing but a simple black bra and matching granny panties looking refreshingly like a real woman, au naturel.

It was her idea.

The article, rare in the magazine industry at the time, centered on the unattainable beauty ideal that magazines play up to, and offered that glam Jamie had been primped and packaged to perfection, then retouched mercilessly for the pages of previous women's books. "In reality," *MORE* proudly exclaimed, "Ms. Curtis has a saggy size-B cup, flabby thighs, and back fat."

Although readers admired the hell out of Jamie for being so brazen, and thanked the *MORE* editors for reminding them that magazine photos are retouched and perfected so the subject looks like Barbie, not much has changed in the magazine industry as a result. What's more, it's only gotten worse. The photos of celebrities and models are regularly retouched in every magazine, making it the new norm; advertisements, as you read in chapter 3, have been banned for doing the same; and celebrities are pampered, glammed up, and styled to appear as gorgeous as they *never* were.

Comedic actress Aisha Tyler underwent a similar epiphany in the pages of a September 2005 issue of *Glamour,* claiming, "I don't want to be Perfect," complete with before and after photos of the retouch, showing readers that celeb women, even the Julia Roberts and the Angelina Jolies of the world, aren't really flawless after all. Ironically, *Glamour*—which has been taken to task often for retouching—asked Aisha to participate in the piece to show how overzealous magazine retouching had become.

Glamour printed not only the before and after versions of Aisha's photos, complete with the original notes of what needed to be retouched, including "brighten and whiten eyes, erase all blemishes and freckles, smooth neck wrinkles, and add cleavage shadows." Who knew cleavage shadows were so desirable?

Aisha wondered in the *Glamour* article if the retouching instructions were over the top for the point of the story, and perhaps so, but she commented that her photos appeared "robot-like," with a glow that didn't radiate from within: "So the next time you see some model or actress with perfect skin, thighs like reeds, and eyes like shimmering pools . . . remember: it's all a big load of digital crap."[9]

Unfortunately, not all magazines step up, nor fess up, when called on the controversial issue of photo retouching. When Kelly Clarkson got a Photoshop diet in the August 2009 edition of *Self,* Editor-in-Chief Lucy Danziger defended it as "art." In a response published on the Self.com blog in August 2009, she wrote: "Portraits like the one we take each month for the cover of *Self* are not supposed to be unedited or a true-to-life snapshot. This is art, creativity, and collaboration. It's not, as in a news photograph, journalism. It is, however, meant to inspire women to want to be their best."[10]

Is it?

Readers similarly went ape-shit over the retouch trim-up of *Ugly Betty* star America Ferrera on the October 2007 cover of *Glamour.* Despite the magazine's denial of digitally altering the star, similar shots of the Latina beauty taken at the same time show her to be quite a bit curvier.

Perhaps *Glamour* would rather dub the show "Skinny Betty."

Despite what we could only imagine were hundreds of disappointed and angry letters to the editor afterward, *Glamour* denied they had slimmed the zaftig actress. Maria Guerra of *Glamour's* reader services responded to several blogger's complaints saying, "Let me assure you, we did not digitally slim her. As she mentions in the interview, she wears a size 6/8 on the bottom, a 10 on the top. You are seeing her as she actually appears."[11]

GLOSSY FACT

When the July 2007 issue of *Redbook* hit stands with a drastically retouched photo of Faith Hill on the cover, popular feminist website Jezebel circulated the original untouched photo of Faith, sending readers into a tizzy over the airbrushed ruse. Former *Redbook* top dog Stacy Morrison told the *Today Show,* "In the end, they're not really photographs. They're images."[12]

Worse was when Oprah Winfrey was asked to appear on the October 1998 cover of *Vogue*. Winfrey spent months whittling herself to *Vogue* Editor-in-Chief Anna Wintour's specifications so she would look suitable in the Steven Meisel-photographed cover. "If you want to be on the cover of *Vogue,* and Anna Wintour says you have to be down to 150 pounds, that's what you gotta do," Winfrey told the BBC. "I didn't think for one moment, 'Now I am going to be a *Vogue* model' nor even did I think I could hold that weight," she confessed.[13]

Oprah looked incredible on the *Vogue* cover, whether it was due to a digital diet or the real thing, no one would say. However, the idea that one of the richest women in the world who made a name for herself empowering other women had diminished herself, both literally and figuratively, simply to appear as a cover girl flew in the face of her feminist ideals, and it contradicted her messages about the power and importance of a woman's self-worth, which she'd been preaching about for over a decade.

Many women know, even accept, that chick slicks perpetuate half-truths and quarter-baked cover lines, and retouch images. And why not? In a world where fudging the truth has become epidemic, where reality TV stars become overnight celebrities, and the *Real Housewives* is one of the most successful television franchise of the decade, it seems just another way the media blurs the fine line between real life and a magazine's airbrushed ideal. Not to mention it upholds a standard to which most of us can't live up to—and don't want to.

Sure, in the media glare of following catty housewives 24/7, making paparazzi-bait out of *The Bachelor* and *Bachelorette* couples, and creating celebrities out of the Kardashian sisters, magazine retouching may not be the worst offense the media commits, but it's up there spiking our blood pressure, insulting our intelligence, and forever disappointing us, if not worse.

Ironically, in the March 2012 issue of *Glamour,* which seems always in the center of the airbrush argument, the magazine took a stand against the practice, asking readers how much is too much. They conducted an independent survey of 1,000 readers, asking them what they thought were "acceptable" elements to photoshop out of images that appeared in magazines. Seventy-seven percent said it was fine to remove blemishes from photos, but only 22 percent were okay with making women appear even five pounds slimmer![14] *Glamour's* big confession was that yes, they airbrush—lightening backgrounds and erasing visible nipples beneath shirts, important work for sure—but they vow in the future to stop the excessive digital manipulation and to tell photographers with whom they work that women's bodies are not to be altered. We can only watch their glossy pages to see if they live up to their "No Airbrush" promises.

Obviously, there's a fantasy factor at play here. If we wanted untouched, unvarnished back flab and sagging breasts, we could just snatch a look in the mirror, or at the very least at our friends and family. The truth is, models and celebrities are packaged like a product by editors, artists, graphic designers, photographers, and writers whose job is to pamper and promote what they're selling, whether that's $100-an-ounce face cream, Manolo Blahnick shoes, or a celebrity's latest movie. It seems editors actually think readers want their cover girls to live up to these impossible standards. Thus, when sales of women's magazines are up, editors assume they are correct in gauging their reader's wants and needs. And when magazine sales go down, as they have been over the past few years, with magazine revenue plummeting from 3.0 to 10.6 percent across the board, editors can blame the recession on lack of sales.[15]

Insider Input

"The images that are being projected to us aren't even real. They are airbrushed manipulations that will keep us chasing the image forever, wondering why we can't measure up. It is so important for us to know the truth, but we can't expect those who most profit from the fabrications to tell us the truth. Because when we are empowered with the truth, we can make different choices. We can vote with our dollars. We can vote with our time . . . Here is the most essential headline women need to read: Nothing is wrong with you. There is no imperfect. You are exactly what this world needs, just as you are."[16]
—Rosie Molinary, author of *Beautiful You: A Daily Guide to Radical Self-Acceptance*

Apparently, the industry doesn't get that readers may be forsaking the glossies not simply because they have less available cash to spend at the newsstand, but because they have less tolerance for perpetuating this unattainable beauty myth.

In fact, some magazines skew so far in favor of the beauty ideal that they often select only the most attractive people for the rest of the magazine, too. Even stories of real women who've had the heart attack at twenty-eight, left their corporate gig and opened a chocolate shop, or lost eighty pounds and ran a marathon aren't captured on the page unless they're sufficiently attractive—or can be retouched accordingly.

Jennifer Romolini, the editor-in-chief of Yahoo! Shine, a U.S. women's lifestyle site, reported that a 2009 issue of French *Elle* showcased several European celebrities without makeup, and said, "American magazine editors, I plead to you: It's time to step up your game. American readers would like to see some real, healthy women who actually look like themselves. We know you slim down their thighs and noses and you lighten their skin. We're tired of fembots. We can handle the truth."[17]

But can we really? Apparently not. Or else why do they keep it up? Why when the letters of praise pour in on features like Jaime Lee Curtis baring it all in *MORE*, or Aisha's digital transforma-

GLOSSY FACT

According to a 2006 survey by the Dove Campaign for Real Beauty Global, 90 percent of women aged fifteen to sixty-four want to change at least one aspect of their appearance, most of all their body weight.[18]

tion in *Glamour*, do they ignore reader's wishes and provide less of those realistic beauty ideals? Oh sure, once in a while they throw in a Jamie or an Aisha who remind us that the models and the actresses within the pages spent six hours in a photo shoot where they were styled, hairdressed, and made faultless, and what wasn't ideal—a tiny zit on their chin, a bit of sag of the breast, a strip of flab along the back of the arm—was wiped away effortlessly by a graphic editor with a computerized retouching program. But not on a monthly basis. And even though we're occasionally tossed a bone, the magazines don't account for the relentless assault of beautiful retouched women who still exist on every other page *in that same issue*—whether the images accompany advertisements or editorial content.

Most serious news organizations have policies against photo manipulation, but not the women's glossies. Here, retouching and slimming models, correcting impurities, and whittling away imperfections are actually the norm. Some claim it's art. Among celeb stylists and publicists, it's more like standard operating procedure.

Yet the real problem with airbrushing is that the standard of beauty is further and further removed from what the average American women's magazine reader can attain. Models weigh about 23 percent less than the average woman, according to a 2004 SizeUSA study.[19] When a celeb or actress is further whittled away by a computer software program, her skin radiantly aglow, her teeth and eyes an unnatural shade of alabaster, the perfect cleavage shadows emanating from her breasts, it may inspire fantasy but it sure doesn't provide readers with any sense of self-significance. After all, if everyone in these pages is so perfect, where does that leave the rest of us?

Maybe we've come too far to turn back.

"Brides are airbrushing the red out of their eyes and getting rid of blemishes in their own wedding photos these days, so the technology's here to stay, but the bottom line is that readers should not be misled," said Cindi Leive, former president of the American Society of Magazine Editors (ASME) and the editor-in-chief of *Glamour,* in a 2008 Daily Beast article.[20]

That may be the case, but it shouldn't apply when it comes to the lady magazines; even *Glamour,* the magazine that Leive knows best, has fallen under such scrutiny on occasion, before their new-found philosophy on retouching. And yet it appears our favorite celebs are regularly transformed into a Stepford image.

In a daring anti-airbrushing video spot by the soap manufacturer Dove, titled "Dove's Evolution of a Model," an ordinary brown-haired woman of average looks is shown being transformed at lightning speed by makeup, hair, and clothes for a mega-billboard cover shot. After the primping is complete, the retouching program begins and the woman who has already gone from ordinary to glam-gorgeous is then retouched via computer brushstroke. Her neck is giraffe elongated, her skin is wiped flawless, her lips are plumped, and her brows lifted—none of it even necessary for the woman, who looks to be in her early twenties. Flash to her billboard photo and the caption, "No wonder our perception of beauty is flawed."[21]

Indeed.

While Dove may appear to be a leader in this anti-airbrush movement with their remarkable Campaign for Real Beauty, even they are not above reproach. In a 2008 *New Yorker* story on premier fashion-photo retoucher Pascal Dangin, the reporter asks him about the Dove ad campaign that shows off "real women" in their undergarments. The photo whisperer, as Dangin's been referred to, says he worked that gig. "Do you know how much retouching was on that?" Dangin asked, implying that it must have been a shit-ton of work getting these cellulite-ridden buxom babes ready for prime time. "But it was great to do, a challenge, to keep everyone's skin and faces showing the mileage but not looking unattractive."[22]

In a joint reply, Dove, its parent company Unilever, and campaign photographer Annie Leibovitz, denied substantially altering the "real women" images. Dangin retracted his earlier statements, claiming they were taken out of context. What's more, Dangin further clarified that he only worked on the 2007 Dove Pro Age campaign, not the original Dove Campaign For Real Beauty ads, in which the *New Yorker* article conjured the images. On the Dove project he worked, Dangin says he performed only minor retouching, such as color correction and dust removal, although that's certainly not the impression we get from his original direct quote.

Regardless, the Dove beauties rocked those photos. But the need for an expert retoucher like Dangin on a project in which all parties claim the goal was not to have a megapixel of retouching

done seems like a whole lot of overkill, no? Why else would they employ the top fashion retoucher in the biz for the photos of the Dove women if any graphic artist on staff could have digitally removed some dust specs?

As for Dangin, he's unabashedly forthcoming in the *New Yorker* piece, acknowledging retouching is a practice clandestinely performed in the dark recesses of a basement workshop. "The people who complain about retouching are the first to say, 'Get this thing off my arm,'" he says, though his very occupation seems to be up for moral, ethical, and philosophical debate.

In March 2008, just months before the *New Yorker* article was published, Dangin tells the reporter he tweaked 144 images for *Vogue*; 107 advertisements for companies like Estée Lauder, Gucci, and Dior; as well as thirty-six fashion pictures, and the *Vogue* cover of Drew Barrymore.[24] He's hired by the advertisers, and photographers such as Leibovitz, and is on retainer for about thirty celebrities. Again, we see the controversial nature of the retouch beast even among celebs that are retouched. While celebrities like Kate Winslet complain about botched retouch jobs (excessive slimming on a cover of the 2008 British *GQ*), other celebrities have professional artist and retoucher Dangin on retainer.

Yet those who sing Dangin's praises realize he's not just a graphic artist with a to-die-for retouch program; rather, he has an innate eye, along with the technical dexterity, to see and create possibilities within a photo that even the photographer couldn't

GLOSSY FACT

Computer scientists at Dartmouth developed a rating system to discern how much airbrushing a photo has undergone. After analyzing nearly five hundred original and retouched images of models, they came up with a mathematical algorithim to analyze photos, using a rating system to show the amount of retouching the photo has undergone (from 1 to 5, with 5 being the most retouched). The researchers' aim? To create a "universal health warning," much like health warnings on a pack of cigarettes, that can be included in magazines. Spurred by their concerns over the negative impact these images have on men, women, and children, researcher Hany Farid said: "Such a rating may provide incentive for publishers and models to reduce some of the more extreme forms of digital retouching that are common today."[26] The results were published in the *Proceedings of the National Academies of Science* in 2011.

capture. Of course, that doesn't mean he's above reproach when it comes to critics who detest a retouch of any type. He admits to spending the majority of his time and effort reshaping an ass, creating a cool dimple, minimizing chubby knees, or wiping away the ropy, veined feet of an over-forty actress in a pair of sexy sandals.[25] And therein lies the fantasy.

Aren't we perpetuating a standard of beauty to which no one can live up to with these images, ones for which the average reader looks at and must ask herself, is this real?

Even Dangin agrees, saying he's only providing the service in response to the request. Supply equals demand. As already pointed out, even some editors-in-chief of women's magazines say that photos aren't even journalism, but instead they are creativity, fantasy, an image to inspire the reader.

Until and unless readers refuse to partake in such images by voicing their complaints or rejecting women's glossies, we suspect Dangin won't have to worry about job security any time soon.

It's clear, despite articles on meditation and intuition, paying it forward, and giving back, women's magazines have little to do with inner beauty, nor really have they ever.

Insider Input

"Retouching has always been a part of . . . glamorous and celebrity-oriented material. . . . People buy magazines like *Vogue* in order to look at a kind of perfection. They are sophisticated enough to know that what they are seeing is a construct. Nowadays people retouch their own snaps on the computer before posting them on Facebook."[27]
—Alexandra Shulman, British *Vogue* editor

Chapter 6

TO AGE OR NOT TO AGE

Beauty isn't an age; it's an attitude.
—Lois Joy Johnson, *MORE* Magazine

One of the biggest problems with aging is that it ages you. Every year that passes you gain a wrinkle, add a sun spot, count another crow's foot, develop batwing flab at the back of your arm, and pooch a little more at the midriff. While the chronological number of your birth comes with newfound wisdom, maturity, and a sense of style and comfort within your own body, your skin pays the price. And not just your skin, but your body, your hair, your teeth, your nails. Face it. None of it looks as good as when we were younger, right?

The bad news is that it happens to all of us. The good news—according to the messages we get from women's glossies—is that advances in cosmetic science have produced an explosion of antiaging remedies: surgeries, needles, lasers, creams, serums, potions, salves, gels, solutions, and yes, scams, to halt the march of time across your face, the downward dog of gravity on your body, and diminish all—well, perhaps most—of the hallmarks of aging.

Every month, these antiaging miracles are touted in articles, advertisements, product reviews, and how-to's. From cover to cover, chick slicks present youthfulness as the beauty ideal, celebrities are lauded for looking young, and cosmetic surgery—once considered an extreme, even taboo pursuit a few decades ago—is now as acceptable as getting a spray tan. The message is clear: youth is the essential elixir of beauty, and it's perfectly acceptable to take whatever measures are necessary to hide aging—if you're a woman. Men, it turns out, enjoy a get-out-of-jail-free card when it comes to showing their years, not just in our culture, but in the dick slicks as well. Not fair! But when you consider that most anti-aging products and services on the market are for women, it's not really a surprise. According to current estimates, it's a $150 billion industry. And since women's magazines are hell-bent on perpetuating a difficult-to-achieve-and-maintain beauty ideal, the cosmetic industry assures itself of those enormous profits.

According to the [cosmetic] industry, age is a disaster that needs to be dealt with, says the Quebec Action Network for Women's Health in its 2001 report *Changements Sociaux en Faveur de la Diversité des Images Corporelles* (Social Changes in Favor of the Diversity of Body Images). If not all women need to lose weight, for sure they're all aging.[1]

And if aging is the enemy, cosmetics are the weapon and the cure. What does that make women's magazines? The Trojan Horse of a woman's positive self-image.

AGEISM IS ALIVE IN THE GLOSSIES

If you're over forty and flip through a copy of *Vogue*, it's rare you'll see anyone your age gracing the cover. While Vogue's readership is one-fifth women over fifty, the only cover girl over forty in 2010 was Halle Berry, who was forty-three when she appeared on the September 2010 cover.

The norm is younger celebrities, including Lady Gaga, Kiera Knightley, Michelle Williams, and Natalie Portman—all in their twenties when they appeared. Worse, a new study finds that the absence of older women isn't just a problem in *Vogue,* or even in women's magazine covers: an analysis of editorial and advertising images reveals that despite demographics of older readers ranging as high as 23 percent, fashion magazines portray women over forty sparingly, if at all.[2] Even in magazines geared toward boomer women, like *MORE* and *Good Housekeeping* the only images portrayed present thin, youthful, wrinkle-free women.

It does lead to problems of negative body image, said study author Denise Lewis, a gerontologist at the University of Georgia who reported the results in the April 2011 issue of the *Journal of Aging Studies*. It leads to issues that have people denying aging and going to great lengths to continue to look like that ideal of a youthful person.[3]

The most age-friendly magazine Lewis found, *Essence,* has a reader base that is 22 percent over age fifty, but only about 9 percent

Insider Input

"I remember being stunned when a *Ladies' Home Journal* editor shared the average age of her mag's audience. It was MUCH older than I expected. Then I tried to figure out why I'd been so off, and I realized it was the pictures in the magazine. None of them seemed to be of anyone over thirty, much less forty."
—Jennifer Fink, writer

of the women on the magazine's pages are over forty. The mag that most closely matched its readership to its photos was *InStyle*, which has an audience that is 11 percent fifty or above. Just fewer than 8 percent of the women in the magazine were over forty.

Even women that we knew to be over forty didn't look like they were over age forty, said Lewis.

Here's how the data broke down by magazine, from most age-friendly to least, reported in LiveScience:[4]

Essence
Proportion of readers over fifty: 22 percent
Proportion of women over forty portrayed: 9.02 percent

Harper's Bazaar
Proportion of readers over fifty: 23 percent
Proportion of women over forty portrayed: 8.75 percent

Glamour
Proportion of readers over fifty: 16 percent
Proportion of women over forty portrayed: 8.65 percent

InStyle
Proportion of readers over fifty: 11 percent
Proportion of women over forty portrayed: 7.93 percent

Vogue
Proportion of readers over fifty: 20 percent
Proportion of women over forty portrayed: 7.33 percent

W
Proportion of readers over fifty: 14 percent
Proportion of women over forty portrayed: 5.09 percent

Cosmopolitan
Proportion of readers over fifty: 9 percent
Proportion of women over forty portrayed: 4.38 percent

Elle
Proportion of readers over fifty: 19 percent
Proportion of women over forty portrayed: 2.68 percent

Of course, women's magazines are all edited by women over, yes, wait for it . . . forty! Let's see, at the time of this writing, the editor of *Real Simple* is forty-six, the editor-in-chief of *Self* is fifty-one, top dog over at *Cosmo* is fifty-nine, *Glamour's* large-and-in-charge is forty-four, *Woman's Day* editor-in-chief is forty-two (but *oops!* she was just replaced before this went to print with a forty-seven-year-old editor), *MORE's* hot mamma is fifty-five, *Marie Claire's* is forty-eight, while *Vogue's* is sixty-two. Enough said?

If you asked these women why they use too-thin models and feature twenty- and thirty-something actresses almost exclusively, they'd probably say that people like looking at youthful images and its presumed equivalent, beauty. Plus, of course, it sells more antiaging serum.

According to a 2008 report titled Market Trends: The U.S. Cosmeceuticals and Antiaging Products Market, the American market for cosmeceutical products is worth nearly $16 billion.[5]

Growth in this category, and the cosmeceuticals market overall, the report asserts, is driven by U.S. consumers who are determined to defy the signs of aging: increasingly, consumers are opening their wallets to purchase a regimen of antiaging products, ranging from standard wrinkle creams to home microdermabrasion kits.

Seems the moisturizing-savvy, alpha hydroxy-loving, hyaluronic acid-injecting women magazine readers believe it's a better investment to buy a $100 eye creme or a $50 plumping lip-liner with revitalizing mineral polymers than funding their 401K or grabbing that fabulous new scarf to wear to dinner. But in all fairness, doesn't it stand to reason that women who are made to feel insecure about aging are more likely to buy beauty products? Absolutely.

And what about the once-taboo topic of plastic surgery? Just a generation ago, it was considered extreme, a fringe procedure limited to facelifts done on wealthy women over sixty. According to the American Society of Aesthetic Plastic Surgery (ASAPS), that's changed. It's become so normalized, they report, that the number of Americans who approve of cosmetic plastic surgeries is increasing, regardless of age and income level. In 2003, for example, nearly nine million people underwent procedures to look younger or enhance their personal appearance.[6]

The survey also revealed that men and women between the ages of eighteen and twenty-four are the most likely to *consider* undergoing procedures themselves, even though the majority of women who actually undergo plastic surgery are between the ages of thirty-five and fifty. Interesting that this is the average demographic of women's magazine readers.

A separate poll of 1,000 women between the ages of eighteen and thirty conducted by the British women's magazine *More!* revealed similar findings. Of those questioned, 72 percent said they want to have cosmetic surgery and 49 percent said they are planning to have work done at some point in the near future.[7] More than half of those who plan future surgeries (57 percent) say they will do so because they are unhappy with the way they look.

If a marketer thinks that the cosmeceutical and antiaging industry is just for the aging Boomer, they should think again, said Don Montuori, editor of the Market Trends Report. "These products . . . are surprisingly popular among young adults, the people one would imagine would have the least use for them."[8]

GLOSSY FACT

In a 2008 survey conducted by *InStyle* magazine titled "What's Age Got to Do with It?" the magazine revealed that readers think Demi Moore and Helen Mirren look great for their age! Forty percent of twenty-year-olds use antiwrinkle creams, and 68 percent of women surveyed insist they are not afraid of aging.[9]

Twenty-four-year-olds now routinely get botox treatments and breast implants—if they haven't done it earlier, that is.

Considering the steady stream of communiqués women's magazines publish every month about beauty and aging, it's no wonder that beautiful-looking women—regardless of age—believe that the female body is an object to be perfected by youthinizing.

Worse, women internalize these stereotypical ideals and judge themselves by the beauty industry's standards. Women learn to compare themselves to other women from magazines, but it's impossible to measure up to the images in the glossy pages.

Readers thought *MORE* magazine might change that. Or maybe not. Launched in 1998 for women over forty, the magazine ran an article on how to appear younger in 2009. Outraging some readers, tips in the piece included learning to text, having a waxed bikini line, and not planning every detail in life.[10] Apparently, the under-forty set doesn't go in much for planning.

Regardless, the slap in the face was apparent. The very magazine lauded for letting women be themselves and catering to content that women over forty might actually enjoy, like what to wear at this midlife juncture, reinventing themselves after divorce, blending families after second marriages, and addressing the health and financial issues of women who've been around the block a time or two, had now jumped the shark, telling women how to appear as though they were younger.

If even *that* magazine is going to tell us how to look, act, and be younger, readers rationalized, then truly what was the point of a magazine for older women? Lesley Jane Seymour, *MORE's* top dog at the time, said they don't take that stuff seriously and they continue to publish features making humorous light about both aging and the inevitable march of time.[11] *MORE's* focus remains assuring Baby Boomer women that they should be their number one priority in their own lives, no matter their age. Yet issue after issue includes an antiaging article.

In fairness, *MORE* emphasizes that the spouse or the kids, or even the career, should all take second string to the woman herself. Women are encouraged to create a work-life balance of gal pals, family, travel, successful financials, fulfilling careers, good health, and love—no matter if that takes the form of a man, a woman, or a good book on a cold night. *MORE* underscores that sex should be about *when the forty-something woman wants it,* and perhaps that her man might just want to please *her* this go round, and for that we can applaud a bit.

Still, *MORE* must battle the war for ad pages and the ever fickle beauty and diet industry among the women's glossies that prohibits them from eschewing diet and antiaging coverage totally. Worse, the antiaging bandwagon starts younger and younger.

THE ANTIAGING OF OUR YOUTH

A few decades ago, skin care—cleansing, toning, and moisturizing so your skin looked clean and pristine—was the norm in magazines like *Seventeen*. Fighting zits was the occasional battle

GLOSSY FACT

According to an online poll conducted by *Allure* magazine, 47 percent of readers say they bought their first antiaging cream in their twenties.[12]

cry, and skin cancer and sunscreen protection were just starting to be bandied about more religiously. Yet now, young women's mags like *Glamour, Cosmo,* and *Self* (magazines for the twenty- and thirty-something set, mind you) have moved on from mere cleansing.

In fact, according to a 2009 *Newsweek* examination of common beauty trends, young girls today start visiting salons at around age eight or nine.[13] Fifth graders have pedicure parties and spa days and regularly head to the hair salon for not just a trim, but things like $150 extensions and highlights. The survey asserts that by the time your ten-year-old is fifty, she'll have spent nearly $300,000 on just her hair and face alone. And by the time she hits the Botox years, the cost of her entire beauty regimen will surpass the cost of a home.

A 2004 survey by the marketing research firm NPD Group showed that on average, women used to begin using beauty products at age seventeen. Today, the average age is thirteen.[14] According to market research firm Experian, 43 percent of six- to nine-year-olds are already using lipstick or lip gloss; 38 percent use hairstyling products; and 12 percent use other cosmetics.[15]

Times sure have changed.

What's caused the beauty revolution among the prepubescent and teen set? Ads for the latest fashions, makeup tips, and grooming products are circulated in magazines, on television—hell, even on Facebook. Girls eleven to fourteen are subjected to some five hundred advertisements a day—the majority of them nipped, tucked, and airbrushed to perfection.[16] And, according to a University of Minnesota study, staring at those airbrushed images from just one to three minutes can have a negative impact on girls' self-esteem.[17] It doesn't help that digital cameras and smartphones come complete with retouching options and apps, and that any computer-savvy girl can learn how to use photoshopping software to blend, tighten, or erase. Long before her features are even fully defined, she's likely adjusting them to unrealistic perfection.

Eight- to twelve-year-olds in this country collectively spend more than $40 million a month on beauty products, and teens spend another $100 million, according to the NPD Group.[18] Cosmetic surgery procedures dipped slightly in 2010, but cosmetic sales have increased between 1 and 46 percent, depending on the product, says the Nielsen Company.[19]

GLOSSY FACT

A 2004 study by the Dove Campaign for Real Beauty found that 42 percent of first- to third-grade girls want to be thinner, while 81 percent of ten-year-olds are afraid of getting fat.[20]

In Susie Orbach's book *Bodies,* the feminist writer and former therapist to Princess Diana argues that good looks and peak fitness no longer are a biological gift, but a ceaseless pursuit.[21] Constant exposure to cosmetic advertising may just cause young girls and women to think they should diet relentlessly and dream about the cosmetic surgery procedures available to them at any age, making their body their sole identity right out of the gate.

Naomi Wolf, author of *The Beauty Myth,* likened the cosmetic industry and their advertising and promotion of beauty products to domestic product and household appliance advertising to propagate the feminine mystique in the fifties, further adding that "the fact that these [antiaging product manufacturers] are some of the major advertisers of mainstream and women's media means that there's very little room to negotiate with the beauty myth within those pages."[22]

If tweens can be convinced they need plastic surgery and twentysomethings think they need Botox, what's left for those of us at thirty, forty, fifty and beyond? Especially as we age with our male counterparts?

DICK SLICKS VERSUS CHICK SLICKS

While women's magazines approach readers as if they were already old—or at the very least need to fight wrinkles at the onset of puberty—men's magazines treat their readers, even the oldest among them, as if they were perpetually and disarmingly young. Why the disparate approach?

In an essay called "The Double Standard of Aging," American literary theorist and political activist Susan Sontag explains how men are much less terrified about aging than women are because there is so much less pressure placed on men to age gracefully. Women, on the other hand, are expected to bathe in the fountain of youth, whatever the cost.

Sontag says being physically attractive counts much more in a woman's life than in a man's, but beauty, identified as it is for women, with youthfulness, does not stand up well to age.[23] Instead of women being valued for professional and personal accomplishments or intellectual growth, they're judged on external beauty standards, whereas a man's esteem and adequacy aren't measured by how handsome he is. On the contrary, older-looking men can be just as manly and attractive, if not more so, because the hallmarks of aging in a man—grey-flecked hair, a lined face—constitute wisdom and competence in our culture, not to mention a distinguished and dapper style. George Clooney is still hot, after all. Clint Eastwood and President Obama only look wiser. Yet what do women get with age, in our culture and others? Plummeting feminine appeal.

Read any dick slick, and this is clear. Take the April 2009 "How to Be A Man" issue of *Esquire,* which opens with an article that outlines all the ways that a real man rocks. Not a single example in this love letter to the attributes of the masculine gender includes references to his attractiveness, weight, or age. In fact, the one reference to age celebrates it rather than qualifies or demeans it: "A man welcomes the coming of age. It frees him. It allows him to assume the upper hand and teaches him when to step aside."[24]

Lucky for the ego of these male readers, it's a recurring theme. In the March 2012 issue of *Esquire,* a feature titled "How a Man Ages . . . or Should," they include forty examples of how to handle aging (in the smart, irreverent writing style that is the hallmark of many men's glossies), beginning at age eighteen and ending at age fifty-eight, fifty-nine, and beyond. Only two—count 'em, two—examples make any reference to aging or beauty, and they're cursory and flip: "Age 42: Worrying that you're starting to look old. Doing something about it."[25] Then there's a brief, almost academic bit of advice about considering using a moisturizer with sunscreen, and how to deal with brown spots or wrinkles. The info is direct, unvarnished, and not couched in any language that suggests there's anything remotely wrong about aging. Nothing about hiding, erasing, looking younger, diminishing your age—all undermining terms that are used regularly with antiaging advertisements and editorial missives in women's magazines. Instead, *Esquire* treats the advice like one might instructions for maintaining your car—as needed: "If you've got lots of brown spots or wrinkles, ask your dermatologist about procedures that get rid of damaged skin cells. Chemical peels work, but a milder alternative is laser technology like the Fraxel laser. It evens out your face's tone and texture without chapping your skin."[26]

The real distinction between how men's and women's magazines treat aging, however, comes in this last bit of antiaging advice. It basically tells men to get over it: "Age 51: Making a big deal about *not* starting to look like your father. Getting used to it."

Wow, chick slicks, you should be *ashamed*.

In fact, though a few of the dick slicks now contain improvement articles: "10 Ways to Get a Six Pack," "How to Stave off Male Pattern Baldness," few if any make aging a regular topic. There simply are no articles about how to hide crow's feet or the products that best remove under-eye bags. There's not a big men's market for cosmetic surgeries either, like brow- and face-lifts, so these story lines are noticeably lean, and washing the gray out of men's hair apparently isn't even an option. That article would more likely be dubbed "Embrace Your Age—Salt & Pepper Is Sexy!" Yet, every single issue of women's magazines contain a diatribe on aging, even though they may be couched in language to make you feel good about your age—whatever it is.

Take a look at the April 2012 lineup of women's magazines: *MORE*, "Best Antiaging Beauty Ideas at 30, 40, 50, 60"; *InStyle*'s "Do They Really Work? Our Panel of Pros Rate Green Beauty Products"; *Elle*, "Your Genius Guide to Everything Beauty: 14 Top Docs, Hairstylists & Makeup Artists Tell Us Which Products & Procedures Really Work"; *Self*, "Give Cellulite the Boot"; *Woman's Day,* "Look Younger Now: Fight Forehead Wrinkles"; *Ladies' Home Journal's* "I'm Too Young to Look This Old"; and *Redbook's* issue with "Forget Praying for Younger Skin: These Things Work."

Yup, they *all* have some reference to antiaging.

It's unfortunate that unlike men's magazines, where editors seem to get that aging can represent a developing wisdom and growth, women's magazines seem to fail at this—even though data shows that women become more creative and independent after age fifty.

Christiane Northrup, MD, a prominent obstetrician and gynecologist and author of *Women's Bodies, Women's Wisdom*, says we associate our forties with loss, but it's really not loss. It's outgrowing. At menopause, the creative sap begins to rise. Women wake up. They have new ideas for businesses; they take on second careers. Around fifty, things really start to get good. The mainstream media teach us that life is over once we're no longer attractive to men. Nothing could be further from the truth. Things get better and better—it's the best kept secret in the world.[27]

Within the realm of women's magazines, however, there have always been rebels. Enter *Beautiful* magazine, a new enterprise for women aged twenty-six to forty-six, trumpeted as totally dedicated to building self-esteem and reversing the damage done by traditional women's media and advertising. *Beautiful*'s founders, Sue Thomason and Sarah Kenny, say their new U.K. monthly will only use models size 12 and over, and have vowed never to publish advice on diets and weight loss.[28] Not that they're excluding

GLOSSY FACT

2010: Year a skin dye called My New Pink Button was marketed to women whose labia have darkened with age. My New Pink Button is described on its website as a simple-to-use genital cosmetic colorant that restores the pink back to a woman's genitals.

smaller-size women, they say, since women come in all shapes and sizes and that's what they aim to replicate on the page.

Thomason says, "I picked up a mainstream women's magazine the other day—not a diet one—and dieting was mentioned eight times on the cover alone."[29]

Beautiful is also shunning ads that harm self-esteem and is embracing the plus-size model. Of course, remember in this industry, plus size might be a mere size 8 or 10, but still, hello zaftig models and actresses, you are once more in vogue.

It's been quite a while since an alternative to the diet-friendly beauty mags picked up a following. Take *Jane*, which, prior to going defunct in 2007, was a smarter, more irreverent, less fluffy magazine that appealed to young women. The brainchild of Jane Pratt, it was the older sister to *Sassy,* which was a hip, spirited feminist magazine for American teenager girls. Pratt was appointed editor-in-chief to *Sassy* in 1988, at the age of twenty-four, before launching *Jane* in 1997.

Both magazines spurned how-to-please-your-boyfriend and look-better-in-your-jeans features in favor of not dieting ever and included unabashed conversations about sex. Yet despite becoming an icon for millions of girls and young women, neither magazine flourished financially and both succumbed to folding.

Now, Pratt has begun a new venture based in New York called www.xoJane.com, a website billed as a place where women can go when they are feeling selfish, and where their selfishness is applauded. It follows her previous mantra—lots of style and sass from women writers, with no mention of making your man happy or whittling your muffin top. Pratt's been tossing around a print publication idea, but has been quoted that it simply hasn't been the right time to launch a new magazine.

* * *

Will these swashbuckling, go-against-the-grain publications thrive in a world where women supposedly want meatier stories and less coverage of airbrushed ideals? It remains to be seen. One thing is clear: women magazine readers are wiser than ever before. Today's readers know when they are being manipulated. They understand that pictures are regularly retouched and that the beauty ideal they read between the perfumed pages is one the cosmetic industry created and the media perpetuates, not one they necessarily have to believe in or aspire to. When looking at any beauty or aging-related content in a women's magazine, women should ask themselves, is it true? Is it realistic? Is it harmful? It's awesome to want to look and feel great, but to what extent women play into the cosmetic bag of goodies and the antiaging medical bag of bullshit being sold to them is still a choice. It's always been a choice, ladies.

Chapter 7

FEMININE FEAR FACTOR

By the time we are women, fear is as familiar to us as air. It is our element. We live in it, we inhale it, we exhale it, and most of the time we do not even notice it.

—Andrea Dworkin, American feminist and writer

It's human nature to be drawn to upsetting and fear-inducing information. All magazines know this, which is why they craft distressing cover headlines using huge colorful fonts and exclamation points. Take recent cover lines from *Cosmopolitan, MORE,* and *Glamour*: "Women and Danger: How This Decision Could Cost You Your Life," "The Migraine Addiction Link: What Your MD Might Be Doing Wrong," and "The Hidden Things Messing Up Your Health: Protect Yourself from the Scary Toxins You Touch Every Day."

Like a mangled car on the freeway or the missing child on a milk carton, we can't look away. Articles that elicit our deepest fears captivate us with crime, terror, danger, disease, toxins, scams, bad doctors, bullies, cyber stalkers, and countless other scary things going on around us. Even if the danger is slight, trumped up, or practically nonexistent, fear sells women's magazines. But at what cost? Are we so fearful of what's printed in the women's magazines that we buy into the printed hype without stopping to consider whether we're being played.

Women's magazine articles (of the lowest common denominator) fall into two categories, occasionally intersecting: the fluffy and the fear-mongering. The former content appears in magazines like *InStyle, Lucky,* and *Glamour,* which fill their pages with articles on the best mascara, Marc Jacob's newest handbags, and gushing reviews of celebrity fashion styles and ecofriendly dog beds. It's generally mindless light reading, hence "fluff," a vapid guilty pleasure. Not so the latter type, which appears in magazines like *Good Housekeeping, Marie Claire, Cosmopolitan,* and *Self.* Their pages are filled with features and first-person pieces on everything from infidelity and infertility to the overblown risks of cell phone use and the likelihood of death by natural disaster. Let's not forget toxic mold and the hidden dangers of the office workplace. Truly scary stuff, and totally compelling reads, which editors know.

The problem is, women's magazines aren't reporting news. Not *breaking* news, anyway. Yet readers assume that these slick glossies are educating and informing them in the same way that our television, newspaper, and online news feeds are. What most of us don't realize, however, is that the writers and editors of these magazines shape, congeal, and generally concoct articles, selecting the facts to include or omit to fit their agenda, which is to sell magazines. Thus, stories are often designed to stoke our fears—even pique our morbid curiosity, which is a form of entertainment in itself—not report the news as it happens, or even to report stories and ideas that are trending.

That's not to say the stories are untrue. Most of them contain excellent, factual information and nuggets of truth, or they're things that *do* happen to some people. But by and by, they may be largely exaggerated, if not intentionally crafted, to sell just the right brand of fearfulness.

Sure there are rare diseases and entire towns that have become a wasteland of poisonous chemicals, but the fear factor is played up more than necessary to draw the reader in and keep her reading. If this happened to that woman, to that family, to that town, couldn't your basement be filled with toxic mold too? Couldn't your doctor's office harbor infectious MRSA bacteria? Couldn't your town be a cancer cluster? Couldn't your very life or that of your spouse or children's be in danger *right this minute?* It's a slippery slope, for sure, but it's one that magazines intentionally push you down.

In one mid-1990s Media Research Center study of thirteen women's magazines, hundreds of features touched on scary social issues, including topics on health and the environment.[1] Deodorant causes breast cancer and too many CAT scans are killing you, endometriosis should be on your radar, as well as the undiagnosed illnesses that kill women across the country. Don't forget doctor misdiagnosis and surgical mistakes!

Women's magazine articles on beating stress, losing weight, medical problems du jour, and violence against women run amok, despite the fact that mortality rates have decreased for women and we're healthier than any other time in history. But women's magazines are ripe for hitting the panic button since women tend to take their stories with a dose of trustfulness and a lion's heart of emotional vulnerability. And because we are generally the gatekeepers of our family's health and well-being, we worry more. In fact, women task themselves with the burden of worrying enough for the whole family.

Researchers at Princeton University and the University of Pennsylvania found that women spend ninety minutes more than men each week worrying, which is more than double the forty minutes a week women spent being unhappier than men at the close of the 1950s.[2] In the 1970s, a brief radical shift occurred, where women's happiness surpassed even that of men—probably in part because the women's movement flourished in the 1970s and '80s. Unfortunately, today's women are back to being unhappy worrywarts—more so even than our mothers. It's not a stretch to point to our media-saturated culture, one that depends on hyped-up headlines and provocative content to draw readers' attention, with women's magazines being right at the front of the fear chain.

THE SLIPPERY SLOPE TO WORRYDOM

So what's the big deal, you might ask, about reading a few alarmist health stories now and then? Certainly, a smart woman gleans from these fear-mongering pieces what is relevant to her and her family, regardless of how alarmist and riveting they are, right? Absolutely. And therein lies the problem. According to a 2009 Missouri School of Journalism study, popular women's magazines tend to focus on what women can do as *individuals* to better their health, yet they largely ignore collective or institutional actions that are needed to address problems in health and healthcare.[3] Researchers suggested that health journalism focusing solely on the individual's role in her health may do a disservice because it turns attention away from government responsibilities and existing inequalities.

"This focus on the individual doesn't leave room for institutional or environmental causes for health problems," says journalism professor Amanda Hinnant, who authored the study. "If the individual has total control, that means the individual has total responsibility for both the cause and the outcome."[4]

Which means women start to worry, because *they* have to shoulder all that responsibility.

The study looked at 148 health articles and cover lines in the nine best-selling women's magazines for March 2004: *Better Homes and Gardens, Good Housekeeping, Family Circle, Woman's Day, Ladies' Home Journal, Cosmo, Glamour, Redbook,* and *O, The Oprah Magazine.* Most articles framed seeking better health as a way of taking control of your life, yet Hinnant suggested this was merely the illusion of control.

"Mood, stress, and energy are frequently substituted as symbols for health. Maintaining good health means constantly patrolling the borders for a bad mood, high stress, and low energy," she wrote. "What materializes is the notion that the pursuit of wellness will result in a life in control, when in fact it is a life that is controlled by the tyranny of constant surveillance."

As if women didn't have enough to worry about, women's magazines expect us to patrol our health in a constant state of vigilance for what we could be doing wrong, what mistakes we're making, what unknown dangers could trip us up, what little-known scan we missed, or what food we forgot to include or omit in our diet for better health. Yet paging through the women's magazines to locate the hidden morsel of danger we've overlooked pretty much defeats the pleasure purpose of the glossy reads.

It's not a stretch to think that even well-meaning campaigns against breast cancer, osteoporosis, and heart disease are designed to fear-monger as well—at least in the way they're sometimes presented in the pages of our magazines. Half their purpose is to educate and inform the reader, while the other is to scare women into thinking that these issues could be just a magazine article away from their lives. Thus, it's incumbent on them to do something about it *themselves,* and often that means buying into a product or service that, conveniently enough, is advertised in those very same pages.

Take osteoporosis. Articles on this bone-sapping disease appear in every woman's magazine, regardless of demographic, alerting women to a disease that emerged from obscurity only two decades before to become one of women's top health concerns. Yet in truth, women are more at risk of a dozen other diseases than having their bones shatter during a tennis match.

Nonetheless, advertising campaigns, brochures, and wall charts in medical exam rooms and pharmacies continually warn women of the dangers of disappearing bone mass. While statistics show that one woman in two over the age of sixty is at risk of osteoporosis, the message we get instead is that once we pass the sixty mark, we're all but likely to crumble from an osteoporotic fracture. Further, we're told that the incidences of hip fractures exceed that of cancer of the breast, cervix, and uterus combined.[5]

These "informative" health articles, which run every few months in women's magazines—like "Bone Up: Strengthen Your Bones and Prevent Osteoporosis" in the March 2012 issue of *Women's Health*—further warn us that 16 percent of patients who suffer a hip fracture will die within six months, and 50 percent will require long-term care. But a study reported in *The American Journal of Health Behavior* looked at osteoporosis articles in women's magazines from 1998 to 2001 and found risk factors and preventive measures were outlined in most articles; however, a lot of the information presented was ambiguous and incomplete.[6] The study concluded that the reporting of osteoporosis in women's magazines and newspapers is not entirely balanced and that future coverage should provide greater detail.

The statistics, the most reliable from The Surgeon General's Report on Nutrition and Health, say that over twenty million Americans have osteoporosis, and that annually, approximately 1.3 million of them will suffer a bone fracture as a result.[7] But it's important to put these statistics into perspective. While it is true that death occurs in men and women who have hip fractures, these people are usually elderly and frail—not at all the demographic of the chick-slick reader. And while tragic, these deaths occur in people who are often suffering from a host of other age-related health disorders.

Yet flip to the health section of any women's magazine and this isn't the takeaway that readers receive. Here, the message is more often what you can do to avoid this fate, offering preventative advice like increasing your calcium intake, pursuing estrogen replacement therapy, and dosing yourself with osteoporosis drugs. Ironic that these three "cures" are often full-page product advertisements in these very magazines, no? But the truth is that your bone density and calcium stores are pretty much set by age thirty, so advice suggesting that loading up on, say, Tums, an antacid tablet touted for its calcium content, will stave off frail bones, is erroneous at best for most women over thirty. According to the Harvard School of Public Health, "Achieving adequate calcium intake and maximizing bone stores during the time when bone is rapidly deposited (up to age thirty) provides an important foundation for the future."[8] Yet we rarely read that our bone density is set by age thirty, and that past that point, we are simply on a path to maintaining our bone health, which most women, save for genetic predisposition and really poor lifestyles, do fairly well. So sure, taking care of your body will pay off as better health in the future (and that's the "informative" half of the article equation mentioned above), but the hyped-up message that women, especially postmenopausal women, will inevitably fall victim to broken bones and crumpled postures is misleading. It implies that you, the reader—regardless of your age, diet, and lifestyle—better take action *now* to protect yourself, and how better to do that than via the products advertised in that very same magazine?

Of course, other articles are downright blatant in their fearmongering, like the story that appeared in the October 2011 issue of *Good Housekeeping*. The magazine pulled out all the scare stops in its health feature titled "Why Your Food Isn't Safe: All of These People Died Because of Something They Ate: How the Safety Net Failed Them—and How to Protect your Family."

Scary, right? Food isn't safe. People died. Here's how to protect your family. Who wouldn't read *that*?

On the first page of the glossy spread, *GH* lists the tragic food-related deaths of twenty people, complete with their photos, birth and death years, and the food that killed them. Eleven of the twenty victims are kids. The other nine are elderly. This, of course, is the demographic hit hardest by food-related illness and death—young children, the elderly, and people with compromised immune systems, but the eleven-page spread doesn't bother to mention that. Nor are those the demographics of *Good Housekeeping.*

Instead, the feature opens with the tragic story of one Iowa teen's horrific ten-day battle with an illness that ends in death via food-borne bacteria, the culprit of which her family has yet to identify. One day she's a normal, healthy kid getting her driver's license and ten days later she's dead, the story points out dramatically.

Who wouldn't be moved and frightened by such a story, particularly as a parent? As moms, women turn to these stories with hearts beating through their chest at the unfairness and devastation of any parent losing their child. It's a mother's worst nightmare, and here it is on the page for your commiseration.

The article uses the teen's story as a launching point to then inform readers about food-contaminated E.coli infections that lead to hemolytic uremic syndrome (HUS), a devastating complication that occurs when E.coli bacteria from contaminated food lodge in the digestive tract and churn out toxins that shred red blood cells, clogging vessels in the kidneys and shutting them down, sometimes fatally.

The piece goes on to list sketchy stats, like those purporting that one in six Americans get sick from something they ate. Seems plausible, yet it doesn't elaborate on the degree of illness. Lots of people get "food poisoning," but after a night spent hugging the toilet (thereby getting rid of the offending source), they're pretty much good to go within twenty-four hours. Not all people—in fact, very few—actually die from food-borne illnesses. And while the article does tell us that three thousand children and adults do die of food-related bacteria, it fails to mention the timetable, whether it's an annual statistic, or if it reflects total deaths since reporting of such cases first began. (A little research revealed that, in fact, most annual deaths occur in adults over age fifty, but the piece fails to mention that.)

The article even points out that the incidents of E.coli have decreased in the United States, but that the biggest decrease was from 1996 to 2000 and there has been little change since. The reader is also reminded of every major food attack and recall in recent history. Sprouts in Germany and France killed forty-seven, ground turkey from Cargill company sickened dozens, romaine lettuce from Freshway Foods caused as many as thirty-three cases of food poisoning, the Jack in the Box restaurant outbreak sickened seven hundred and killed four, and the Country Cottage restaurant occurrence in Locust Grove, Oklahoma, killed one. Death by peanut butter is remembered, as well as the Veggie Booty snack recall that left dozens of mostly young children ill in twenty-three states.

But stop for a minute and put this in perspective. It's estimated that two thousand people worldwide get hit by lightning annually, and we don't exactly consider that a run-of-the-mill occurrence. Yet this article implies we are all just a cheeseburger away from food poisoning, and a cheese curl away from death.

From here, readers of the article learn that the FDA only inspects a mere two percent of imported produce from around the world—like tomatoes, onions, and cantaloupes–suggesting that the bulk of these imported fruits and veggies are loaded with undetected diseases and bacteria just waiting to sicken us. Yet no one mentions that lettuce purchased from your local farmer's market or roadside fruit stand may also be laden with bacteria.

Most of these "alarming" examples of risk are bolstered by tragic stories of victims who either died as a result, suffered serious illness, or were left with permanent poor health and a lengthy list of chronic health problems, such as lethargy, weakness, high blood pressure, chronic kidney disease, and more.

We learn about the six major strains of E.coli, some more deadly today than ever before, and how bureaucracy keeps the government from taking the action to make sure these contaminants don't end up in our beef, cheese, and produce while more people die.

The article then quickly turns to the question of why the government has not been able to eliminate E.coli from the food supply. We're told food regulation is haphazard at best, liable at worst, and held together by a patchwork of inspections and investigations from different agencies—the entire system filled with holes, making the infrastructure weak—much like the fragile bones of a late-stage osteoporosis patient.

"The USDA is responsible for overseeing the cows, while the FDA is in charge of the milk," the article states. Pepperoni on pizza? That's the USDA's oversight. But cheese pizza is regulated by the FDA—and so on.

The numbers are dizzying. Not only is money at the root of the problem, naturally, with many figures provided, but the number of staff at both organizations is too lean. We hear about the number of food manufacturers, warehouses, slaughterhouses, and processing plants in this country. Then we're shown the pathetically low number of staff assigned from each of the agency's available pool of regulators to inspect and investigate each of these entities, and our eyes cross. What the heck number corresponds with what the heck entity being discussed? It's hard to discern! All we know is it's bad, very bad. It's scary. Very scary.

Is this story the truth? Hell yes, it's true. By and large. Have innocent people been sickened and killed? Of course. Is it heart-wrenching and terrifying that any of us can be taken out after eating a fucking salad, or giving a healthy puffed rice snack to our toddler? *Ugh*, absolutely. And women's magazines must know this because these stories are often crafted in a way that scares the shit out of readers, in this case to make women think twice about every burger they're yet to wolf down, or bean sprouts they're yet to buy at the grocery store. And the bottom line, yet again, the article asks, is whose fault is it? And how can *we*, the reader, ever fix this horrid situation? Here, the writers help us along, raising the alarm further by calling for a grassroots movement (because, as the article pointed out, our federal agencies are inept to protect us), and then, just to really hammer it home, the story offers up more scary details in sidebars and pullout boxes, listing the "top eleven foods that can hurt you" along the bottom of one page. The problem is that nearly every food listed is something people eat on a regular basis, (beef, dairy, fruit, fish, beans) ones they probably wouldn't eliminate from their family's diet. And the whole thing is packaged up properly, telling readers what they "need to know." It omits what doesn't work for the story, like how rare it truly is to be killed eating a hamburger, leading readers into thinking that one out of every handful of people could be killed today via a fast food meal—or a tomato! Hell, by nearly any food, really. Yet the statistics aren't that far off lightning strikes, and we don't generally obsess about protecting ourselves from outdoor electrocution.

Nor is fear relegated only to health issues. It lurks in plenty of lifestyle stories. In the October 2011 issue of *Women's Health,* an article titled "The Maybe Baby Mindset," subtitled "When It Comes to Getting Pregnant, More Women Are Letting Fate Decide, But Experts Say That Kind of Ambivalence Might Put You—and Your Potential Offspring—in Harm's Way," sums up the mild hysteria we see packaged month in and month out in women's glossies.

The gist of this particular story is that many women aren't actively trying to get pregnant, but they also aren't really preventing it. Women with this "maybe I'll have a baby" attitude have now outnumbered those actively trying to get preggers, says a "new study." It's important to note that "studies" are gold in *any* article because they lend credibility to stories, but the reader is rarely given the context or the study parameters, many of which can be flawed, narrow, or totally biased. Healthy skepticism goes a long way. Worse, the article goes on to showcase how this laissez-faire attitude can wreak havoc on you and your future progeny's very health and happiness. The piece goes so far as to imply that women are actually scared of making the decision to get pregnant, so this newfangled take-it-or-leave-it attitude about whether they'll roll the dice on parenthood is a fear-based move. "Choosing not to choose allows women to skirt the nerve-wracking 'Am I ready for kids?' question and emotional process of trying to conceive," the piece asserts. It's not clear how the writer came to that conclusion, however. It's the magazine's interpretation of the study material, and pure conjecture, backed up by no real women examples who claim they're afraid of making the parenting decision.

The article waxes on about how women with unplanned pregnancies are less likely to receive early prenatal care, thereby putting their baby's health in jeopardy. It even suggests that women who have a blasé attitude about motherhood may also be tempting the prenatal gods: Since they're likely not aware they're pregnant right away, they may eat, drink, and engage in some degree of bad-for-pregnancy habits (soft cheese, downhill skiing, Long Island Iced Tea?), like one woman in the story who spent the first months of her "undecided" pregnancy hoping she hadn't harmed her little half-planned baby by indulging in too much vino on vacay before she knew she had conceived.

The issue with stories like these is that they skew the statistics of a perfectly good study to fit the alarmist angle they're trying to sell you. When in fact, the study is taken totally out of context to support this "maybe I'll get pregnant" attitude the whole piece is about. In this case, they took a study of four thousand women between the ages of twenty-five and forty-five years old, of which 71 percent reported they were not trying to get knocked up, 6 percent reported they were trying, and 23 percent swore they were okay either way. The study only gives us the numbers. But the article purposefully crafts those numbers into a "one in four women are pretty much wishy-washy and/or afraid of making a decision about pregnancy" statistic, which the author uses to showcase this group of women—this one in four stat—making the leap that their future babies could very well be at risk of inadequate prenatal care. After all, she did say she was okay either way, which implies that to her, being a mom is a half-hearted ideal at best. And if it's not a big deal to these women, the conclusion is that she and her offspring may actually be in real peril. And who is responsible? She is, yet again.

Dating and relationship topics are fodder for fear mongering as well. In the October 2011 issue of *Marie Claire*, a relationship piece on what men won't reveal until the third date scares the shit out of single women by proffering up six men who all reveal the magazine's version of a relationship deal-breaking secret. The men in the piece admit to things like "I am a recovering alcoholic" and "I did time in the clink." Sobering candor, to be sure. The type that implies a woman's dating pool is filled with men who tell lies and hidden half truths that will undermine her chances at love. Talk about discouraging.

But this is nothing compared to the terror-inducing stories of true crimes against women.

SAFETY ADVICE COUCHED IN CRIME STORIES

In the November 2011 issue of *Cosmo*, there's a feature titled "How Serial Killers Choose Their Victims." Great. The ubiquitous rapist hiding in every bush has now been usurped by a new villain in town: the serial killer. Of course you have to read it. Who wouldn't, because the title implies that you, dear reader, are his next victim. And then the piece supports this suggestion by offering up "safety tips" on how you can avoid being vulnerable to a serial killer, as if he's a spring virus waiting to catch you with your guard down. Worse, this terrorfest is accompanied by grisly facts and details about real cases of women who've fallen prey to a serial murderer. Tragic and horrifying, to be sure, but will most readers ever encounter a serial killer? Unlikely. The FBI reports that "serial murder is a relatively rare event, estimated to comprise less than 1 percent of all murders committed in any given year. However, there is a macabre interest in the topic that far exceeds its scope and has generated countless articles, books, and movies."[9] That includes the women's mags that prey on women's fear of such horrific crimes.

GLOSSY FACT

Women are more likely to be victimized by someone they know than by a stranger.

—U.S. Deptartment of Justice

Of course, the piece recounts dozens of instances where women were brutalized and murdered by serial killers, including the Baton Rouge Serial Killer, the Cabbie Killer, BTK (bind, torture, kill), the Bike Path Killer, and the Truck Stop Murderer. These horrific nicknames aren't lost on readers either, making each one loom larger. Underlying it all and weaved throughout the article is the advice portion, where women are schooled on how a serial killer may scope his victims, including casing her home, following her from work, learning her routine, hoping she'll ignore instincts and gut feelings, flattering her, and offering to make her a model or an actress. One serial killer, it goes on to say, even set a trap on a victim's street by putting tire-popping spikes on the road so he could ambush her while she changed her tire. Though we're not sure how any woman can prevent that occurrence, the true advice would be to stay in your locked vehicle and call for immediate assistance, but the piece ironically skips sharing that tidbit. The three-page spread is complete with photos of both victims and killers, a diagram of the box route you should drive if you suspect you're being followed (three consecutive right turns), as well as a sidebar on signs that you may be dealing with a psychopath (excellent advice for any woman).

However, the entire piece gives you the feeling that you're one abduction shy of being stalked by a serial killer. Is there any real

Insider Input

"Women's magazines approach crime stories like it's Armageddon and they're the first ones to find out about it. Sure, there are things women should know about crime and how to protect themselves, but in general, magazines are not interested in conveying information. Instead, their primary concern is to sell magazines, and if it takes scaremongering and/or blaming the victim to do that, then most magazines are fine with it. . . . *Marie Claire* is where you go to walk off the weight, not learn how to save your ass if you're assaulted."

—Carole Moore, author of *The Last Place You'd Look: True Stories of Missing Persons and the People Who Search for Them* value here? It doesn't seem so, since we know—from the story—that serial killings make up less than one percent of murders. Wouldn't a straight-up story on how to protect yourself from crime, in general, be more useful? But where's the shock value in that?

In another questionable *Cosmo* article in the February 2012 issue, the story titled "How Smart Women Put Themselves at Risk" is even more terror-inducing because it highlights the cases of several assaults, abductions, and murders and tells us what each of the female victims possibly did wrong. It's written by a former sex-crimes prosecutor turned novelist, which may explain the tone—more murder-mayhem material than serious safety advice. The article tells us there's been a number of women disappearing in the headlines, many of whom are later found in shallow graves or dumpsters, and others who are never located. It then goes on to outline the possible missteps each of the victims might have made, which ended her life. Mistakes like ditching your friends while out, not struggling with an abductor, and having a public altercation with your partner, leaving you vulnerable to a nearby predator.

Not only does the piece seem to blame the victim by suggesting she wouldn't have fallen prey if she'd behaved differently, but the thinly veiled advice is hidden within the story. Unfortunately, these types of "articles" do more harm than any possible good for women.

One Florida State University study confirms this. Researchers looked at how TV coverage of the sexual assault and murder of two teenage girls in Houston affected viewers' fear of crime, gathering their data in the immediate aftermath of the media frenzy about violent crime, gang violence, and related topics. The study showed that the only demographic that experienced an elevated fear of crime after watching these news stories was middle-aged white women. Nonwhite women and all men, despite being statistically more likely to be victimized, did not become more fearful.[10] The researchers suggested that Caucasian women substitute media coverage for direct experience of victimization, meaning that a person's prior experience with crime—even just *knowledge* of a victim—is a strong predictor of their fear of becoming a victim. Seems white women who watch the news see a disproportionate number of white female victims, leading to a perception that white women are in much more danger than they actually are. This phenomenon has been dubbed Missing White Woman Syndrome.[11]

GLOSSY FACT

Between 1990 and 1998, the murder rate in the United States decreased by 20 percent. During that same period, the number of stories about murder on network newscasts increased by 600 percent. Frequent viewers of evening newscasts were unlikely to have the impression that the crime rate was dropping.[12]

—U.S. Department of Justice

The message is that TV and print media stories can influence our perceptions of ourselves and the world around us. And since white female victims are deemed the most newsworthy (clearly the only newsworthy crime victims in women's magazines), this media coverage can only skew our perceptions of how risky our lives are, and who exactly needs increased protection from criminals.

WHAT DOES FEAR-MONGERING SAY ABOUT US?

Women have always gravitated to stories about other women's problems. It's a complex psychological lure, and it's been a staple of magazine journalism from the beginning. Reading the plight of women victims—whether they have been demoralized by the system or sickened by a rare illness—stokes our empathy and allows us to put ourselves in her shoes. *There but for the grace of God go I!* we think. We're suddenly more fastidious about hand washing, what we eat, who we date, how we drive, even how we *live*.

Yet readers tend to see the messages of these fear stories as an endless loop circling them, and while often the facts are intact, the bottom line is that most articles are driven by the end goal of providing a market for advertisers. The resulting scare stories are partly intentional, because once readers feel the fear, they're motivated to reduce it, often by buying the products advertised in the surrounding pages, or even just by turning to next month's issue for more information about the latest fear factor coming down the pike. There's a level of self-satisfaction we receive in being able to control our world by informing ourselves; we're protecting our loved ones and staying on top of the issues. It's a never-ending cycle of fear-induced loyalty to these publications: if we stop reading them, what might we miss out on?

Yet while most people avoid situations in life where there is real risk of actual injury, we enjoy the experience of being scared in a seemingly safe environment, like visiting a haunted house—or riding a thrilling roller coaster. That's all well and good. Who doesn't like to be entertained when we know we'll come out safe at the other end? The issue becomes more complex when we, as readers, empathize deeply, and then react to the material (either living in a heightened state of fear or buying/subscribing to products or services we probably don't need).

To illustrate, consider the following experiment, conducted by Harvard University and University of Chicago: law students were asked what they would be willing to pay to avoid a one-in-a-million cancer risk. They could check off $0, $25, $50, $100, $200, $400, or $800 or more. One set of students was asked the question in a direct, unemotional way, while the other was given a substantially more vivid description of how gruesome and devastating cancer can be, and *then* they were asked to report the value they would pay to avoid it. The unemotional group averaged about $60 to avoid a one-in-a-million risk of cancer, while the emotional group averaged $210, nearly four times as much.[13] The study, published in the journal of *Environmental and Resource Economics,* found that much of the time, most people will focus on the emotionally perceived severity of the outcome, rather than on its likelihood.

The study suggests that when it comes to actual injury or harm, vivid images and concrete pictures of disaster can "crowd out" the cognitive activity required to consider that the probability of disaster is really quite small.

Women's magazines are pros at capitalizing on this "crowding out" phenomenon. For every article on a rare or seemingly innocuous topic, there are vivid descriptions and heart-wrenching or fear-inducing photos accompanying it. The message to readers is clear: this could happen to *you.* Aren't you afraid?

So, are we victims or victors? Well, we're both. We feel victorious to be informed against risk, even touting our knowledge to friends, feeling self-satisfied and responsible for doing something about it (like buying unnecessary products and supplements; or taking unnecessary preventive actions, like eliminating perfectly good spinach from our family's diet, or ditching our daily morning run in the park).

Yet the overriding mission of women's magazines is not really to educate and inform; it's to sell more magazines (which is the "victim" part of the equation here). To really learn about breast cancer or food-related E.coli bacteria, readers wouldn't crack open *Good Housekeeping* or *Glamour* to get such information, especially when the topic is alarming or fear-producing. There's also nothing wrong with holding women's magazines accountable when article content focuses on thinly veiled infomercials, rare disorders, or fear-factor oddities that likely won't happen to most of us. Are many single women going to encounter a date who has worked as a male prostitute, *Marie Claire*? Probably not.

But don't hold your breath that it will change anytime soon. Magazines know what they are striving for, and fear sells much more effectively to women than we might think. Ultimately, it's up to us (yes, once again, we're the controllers of our fate) to decide if we'll buy into fear-mongering stories, or if we approach them with a healthy dose of skepticism, sussing out the grains of truth and wisdom in between the lines of hype and hyperbole, and refuse to succumb to the fear. Refusing to be a victim is the only way we'll outsmart fear-mongering in the pages of women's glossies.

Chapter 8

TO THE LEFT

In politics if you want anything said, ask a man.
If you want anything done, ask a woman.
—Margaret Thatcher, British Prime Minister

D espite the shortcomings of women's magazines—from their airbrushed ideals and youth-obsessed focus to their lack of transparency and plethora of fluff, you may be surprised to know that women's magazines consistently, with a few caveats, value women politically. In fact, a host of issues important to women— from domestic abuse to pay equality and reproductive rights— continue to get the attention they deserve, politically and socially, thanks to women's magazines.

Month in and month out, glossies as different as *Ladies' Home Journal* and *Vogue* also give voice to real women, regularly featuring intimate stories of everyday women standing up for themselves or others. Whether the pieces are about launching grassroots campaigns, providing resources to underserved women, or exposing systemic abuses against women here and abroad, such issue-oriented stories galvanize and inspire readers, particularly when the articles and profiles focus on issues that readers find important. However, some critics argue that the editorial content and perspectives of these magazines are skewed to the interests of a selective audience, a liberal one, giving short-shrift to the perspectives and ideals of more conservative readers, particularly when it comes to reporting on conservative female politicians. And therein lies the rub, because haven't we been aiming to get a woman into the White House for decades? Talk about a cover story. Tea Party, Green Party, Democrat, or Republican, a woman in the Oval Office is a win-win for women overall—or so we assume. So how do women's magazines—which are part of our liberal media—herald the achievements of these conservative women (like Sarah Palin or Michele Bachmann), who are against many issues championed by these same magazines? And are women's glossies also guilty of marginalizing women politicians across the board, focusing on hearth-and-home issues instead of broader politics, like foreign affairs and the economy? Many would argue that yes, they are. Let's take a look.

COVERING THE CANDIDATES

One perceived problem with the political coverage in the glossies is that the very stories meant to inform and educate us on the issues or introduce us to the movers and shakers of the game are merely dumbed-down fluff masquerading as women's political agenda. A 2010 Purdue University paper titled "Media Coverage of Women in Politics: The Curious Case of Sarah Palin" found that discussions of political women tend to focus on rather trivial subjects such as their physical appearance, lifestyle, and family rather than their positions on prominent campaign issues.[1]

For instance, during the 2008 election cycle we watched as cable news legal-eagle Greta Van Susteren asked Sarah Palin if she had breast implants on live TV. Nancy Pelosi, the highest-ranking female politician in American history, shared that upon entering into politics she was frequently asked who was watching her children—as if a male politician would ever be asked who's at home with the kids. Let's not forget Hillary Clinton and the ugly pantsuit debacle that was the talk of her 2008 campaign. At one Clinton event, people in the crowd heckled her with "Iron my shirt, Iron my shirt!" a blatantly sexist dig insinuating that Hilary should leave the politics to men and get her trouser-clad-ass back to the kitchen where she belonged. Of course, Hillary was further out of the kitchen than most female politicians we know, having had her own law career, eight years as America's First Lady, and a stint as a U.S. senator. And that was *before* she was appointed secretary of state in 2008. Worse, pundits said she had a shrill or castrating voice, implying she was a nagging woman that men couldn't—or wouldn't—tolerate listening to for four years if she were elected president.

Going back even further, Elizabeth Dole was criticized for her schoolmarm appearance, while the first female vice-presidential candidate, Geraldine Ferraro, was once introduced as "Geraldine Ferraro, size 6"! Can you imagine introducing Dick Cheney as "Dick Cheney, size 44-inch waist"?

Yet sadly, in an October 2012 *Vogue* profile of New York Senator Kirsten Gillibrand, the writer goes right for the weight-loss jugular, asking, "How much did you lose?" And here's how the exchange goes down:[2]

"Should I tell you? Really?" Gillibrand asks.

"I really want to know," pushes the interviewer.

"Can I tell you off the record?"

"The readers of *Vogue* will want to know this." (Now he's relentless.)

"Oh, all right," she says. "I will tell you. I lost over forty pounds."

Wow.

With Sarah Palin, the media employed a different tactic. If they couldn't accuse her of being shrill, unstylish, or lacking maternal instinct, they had to find some other way to devalue her. So they attacked not just her inexperience and ignorance—which were valid areas of scrutiny—but worse, they also suggested that her femininity and attractiveness undermined her credibility as a vice-presidential candidate. Comedian Tracey Morgan called her "good masturbation material," and Palin was "pornified," a term first bantered around after a 2011 study that appeared in the journal *Sexuality and Culture*. The study analyzed one thousand *Rolling Stone* images over forty-three years and found among those images that were sexualized, 2 percent of men and 61 percent of women were hypersexualized, meaning intensely sexualized or "pornified."[4] The media also "ditzafied" Palin every time she made an error or public gaffe as a way to devalue an attractive political woman by referring to her as a ditz.

According to the Purdue study, women's magazines weren't necessarily exempt from these sexist traps either. During the 2008 election cycle, for example, while some glossies did cover Palin, others embraced a different sort of political snobbery. Rosemary Ellis, editor-in-chief of *Good Housekeeping,* was quoted as saying, "We have no plans to speak with Governor Palin before the election, but when it's all over, maybe we'll invite her to tour the legendary Good Housekeeping Research Institute, where she can test out the zero-degree temperatures of our climatology room. It might be a welcome change after such a heated race."[5]

Talk about an Alaskan deep freeze!

And yet to the extent that women's magazines *did* cover Palin's political positions, they mostly concentrated on topics traditionally thought to be women's issues, such as reproductive rights, childcare, the environment, and education.

While these topics are important and relevant to us as women, we also have an interest and stake in matters like national security, the economy, and military affairs, which have long been considered the province of men. By not covering these topics to the same degree they do "women's issues," the glossy slicks perpetuate this sexist marginalization. And when the media focuses so fiercely on the appearance of women in politics, it not only trivializes them, but also, by association, every other woman in America. The 2011 documentary *Miss Representation,* depicting how the media's misrepresentation of women leads to the underrepresentation of women in power, pointed out that this robs women of their sense of political efficacy, the feeling that their vote matters, their voice counts, and their choice can make a difference.[6]

The sexism of the 2008 campaign still resonates, but kudos to women's magazines, like *MORE,* for focusing a more thoughtful—if not somewhat politically biased—lens on the topic. In their December 2011/January 2012 issue, they ran a feature titled "Running (for President) in Heels," which looked at sexism among women candidates. The article rehashes how Hillary played down her sexuality in manly pantsuits of subdued colors, never mentioning her femininity, motherhood, or even that she would be the first female president if she won. Whereas Palin, by comparison, was said to have leveraged her femininity and motherhood and played up her sexuality. With her rimless spectacles, red lipstick, and skirts that accentuated her curves and shapely legs, she was the hot-teacher fantasy to countless male supporters, who dubbed her a MILF (Mother I'd Like to Fuck). While this certainly speaks to the weakness of men, not women, her attractiveness and sex appeal, the article asserts, were considered an inherent fault of *hers*. Consider the flip side: had President Obama's sophisticated good looks and trim physique been admired in equal measure during the election, they'd likely be considered strengths rather than weaknesses. It's the classic double standard of sexism.

When the *MORE* piece finally turns to Bachmann, we learn she was of a different ilk than either of her predecessors, not hiding nor flaunting her sex appeal. Rather than Hillary never mentioning motherhood and Palin parading her children around like bait at feeding time, Bachmann takes a middle ground, mentioning motherhood as just one positive thing she's accomplished. (She puts Angelina Jolie's mommy skills to shame, having raised five children—three daughters and two sons—and twenty-three foster children, all girls.)

Yet for all the comparisons the piece makes, and all the legitimate questions it raises about the degree to which we portray our women candidates in a sexualized light, the reporter's liberal bias comes through when she informs readers that she was hoping to get a comment about Bachmann from various prominent political women, but none would talk to her. Palin is unreachable, Elizabeth Dole takes a pass, Condoleezza Rice politely declines, and Liz Cheney is too busy. The piece wraps up asking why not one single woman could offer up a comment on Bachmann. Not even her Republican brethren could be bothered. The implication is that something must be fundamentally wrong with this woman. After all, she is an extreme social conservative, the story reminds us.

While it smacks of bias on the surface, there is the real fact that Bachmann takes a hard line against many of the issues important to *MORE's* readers, issues that represent rights, freedoms, and gender equity. Thus, the publication has some responsibility in alerting readers to this fact. In light of that, *MORE's* gentle treatment of Bachmann could be considered more balanced than on first blush.

GLOSSY FACT

In the U.S. House of Representatives, there are currently 362 men and 76 women. In the Senate, there are 17 women and 83 men.[7]

In fact, *MORE* consistently attempted a mature and balanced view of conservative women, despite their left-leaning political affiliation. In an earlier May 2011 issue, the magazine ran a feature titled, "It Doesn't Matter What Sarah Palin Does or Even Whether Michele Bachmann Runs. What Matters Is That Thousands of Conservative Women Are Connecting with Their Female Candidates—and Each Other—with Unexpected Passion." The article examined the movement of conservative women, dubbed "Mommy Patriots," who followed Palin, Bachmann, and frankly any conservative women in politics. The reporter follows a contingent of conservative moms who are headed to Washington,

D.C., for a rally to protest the healthcare bill. We meet several women along the way and hear of their conservative roots or the fact that they were galvanized into political activism after becoming critical of Obama. The article shares these women's viewpoints, and while more liberal readers may not agree with them, the story nonetheless provides an intimate look at the power of women coming together politically.

Still, the slight liberal bias can't be mistaken. The reporter mentions that they pass out "Impeach Obama stickers" and debate the government's ownership of newborn bloodspots and baby DNA warehousing, a program started in the 1960s for screening genetic birth defects and diseases, which prompts the women to worry about "government cloning." It's implied that these conservative women, and by default their Tea Party candidates, sound a little off-kilter.

However, *MORE* tries to set the bar higher by avoiding the sexist traps of the 2008 election cycle.

In the February 2012 issue, for example, First Lady Michelle Obama graces the cover in her heart-friendly red dress, in a story titled "Michelle Obama Gets Personal." The seven-page article avoids falling into trite questions about what goes on in the White House kitchen or how she chooses her weekly wardrobe. Absent, too, is any partisan messaging. Instead, we read about a mentoring program for high school girls that any woman along the political spectrum can get behind. Much like the nationwide Big Brother/ Big Sister program for underserved youth, the First Lady's program taps female White House staffers interested in mentoring and matches them with local high school girls—the ones that fall in the middle of the spectrum and often get overlooked because they're either not high-risk enough or not high-achieving enough. The focus is on providing role models, and teaching these young women-to-be how to network. Girls can chat up Supreme Court justices or head over to the Department of Labor to learn about landing a job in a tough market.

While the story naturally veers slightly into Mrs. Obama's upbringing and her experiences at Princeton, the article truly sticks to its core: the mentorship program and how senior women of the White House, like senior adviser Valerie Jarrett and former Social Secretary Desirée Rogers, can make a difference in the lives of young women. Free of policy issues and partisan rhetoric, the article instead captures the essence of the program, one that's inspiring to readers of any political ilk. Refreshingly, *MORE* is not the only glossy girl-mag that's begun shifting to a more balanced approach, free of sexist pitfalls, when profiling female politicians.

The February 2012 issue of *Marie Claire*, for example, featured an unbiased profile of Nikki Haley, the Republican governor of South Carolina. The two-page spread was more than flattering to the South Carolina governor, who at age forty is the youngest-serving U.S. governor and South Carolina's first female chief executive. Born to Punjabi immigrants, and only the second governor of Indian descent in the United States, the piece chronicles Haley's discrimination from childhood and what's helped her get ahead, and avoids any talk of where the governor stands politically on policy-related issues.

Absent also is any reference to what the governor wears, looks like, or whether she hides or flaunts her sexuality; nor does it utter a word about her marital status or her thoughts on motherhood. Redlisted as a possible presidential contender in 2016, Haley is lauded for getting to the top of her game. What's more, the article continues, she inspired women everywhere by crushing her ubersexist male opponent during the election when she discovered a published quote from him so chauvinistic and backward, it could have been a script line from *Mad Men:* "Women are best suited for secretarial work, decorating cakes, and counter sales, like selling lingerie." Her campaign dropped that beauty in a flyer and mailed it out across the state. Women in South Carolina were furious, and Haley got herself elected.

Liberal or conservative, what woman among us wouldn't high-five Haley for such a bold, prowoman act? The article serves to unify, not polarize, women. Kudos to *Marie Claire* for that.

POLITICAL COVERAGE IN THE CHICK SLICKS

Historically, women's magazines have gradually increased their coverage of political issues, particularly those with social significance as they relate to women. Today, political pieces in our glossies include not only social issues of our time but also profiles of candidates and their political platforms, and deeper investigation of topics of debate between candidates from different sides of the political spectrum.

A paper published in *The Journal of Psychology*, titled "The Representation of Women's Roles in Women's Magazines over the Past 30 Years," bears this out. It found that political and social awareness topics in *Ladies' Home Journal* and *Good Housekeeping* increased approximately 3 percent from 1954 to 1962, 10 percent between 1964 and 1972, and 18 percent between 1974 and 1982.[8] The research also shows that political and social awareness topics generally increased after political events. For instance, a 1969 piece titled "Trespass" in *Ladies' Home Journal* about a confrontation between rich whites and revolutionary blacks ran a year after the race riots following Martin Luther King's assassination, and an article "The Day J.F.K. Died" appeared in *LHJ* in 1968 on the five-year anniversary of Kennedy's assassination.[9]

Yet besides the fact that these traditional women's magazines increased their political coverage threefold from the 1950s, their focus no doubt remains on traditional women's topics such as homemaking, beauty, health, and sometimes parenting. To look through today's magazines, the range of products being advertised hasn't changed all that much, only the ad campaigns have been updated and new brands have cropped up. It's no wonder, then, that a little political coverage goes a long way when it comes to the traditions of the women's magazines. Editors still mustn't antagonize their advertising revenue stream with articles that stray too far from women's assigned gender roles.

Readers Respond

"Wait, what? Women's magazines cover political issues?"
—Sandra, writer and editor

In fact, Canadian journalist Jenn Goddu studied newspaper and magazine coverage of three women's lobby groups from 1980 to 1995 and revealed that journalists focused on the homes and families of the candidate's life (such as "details about the high heels stashed in her bag, her napping habit, and her lack of concern about whether or not she is considered ladylike"), rather than her position on the issues.[10]

Of course when it comes to politics, the real groundbreaker in the circle of women's magazines was *Ms.,* which was thought to be both wildly radical and boldly brazen in its political coverage. From the first issue with "Welfare Is a Women's Issue" (Spring 1972) to "Women Voters Can't Be Trusted" (July 1972), "Why Women Voted for Richard Nixon" (March 1973), "The Ferraro Factor: What Difference Can One Woman Make?" (October 1984) to

"Hillary in the Crossfire" (July 2000), *Ms.* never backed off their political coverage. And *Ms.* did something else nervy: it put real political women on its cover. Their cover girls were sought out for being women who've made a difference, not simply for being beautiful. Cover girls included Helen Gahagan Douglas (congresswoman, 1945–51), Shirley Chisholm (first black woman in Congress), and Bella Abzug (congresswoman, 1971–77).

In fact, *Ms.* magazine's leap into the political arena galvanized other women's magazines to up their political ante in one fashion or another. Doors opened, boundaries were pushed, and women became more educated and active in social, political, and foreign affairs. Women's magazines took note and today many try to include harder-hitting political stories amid all the fluffy content and airbrushed pages.

Insider Input

Details Editor-in-Chief Dan Peres, upon being asked which women's magazine he'd edit, said: "I'm kind of waiting for Cindi [Leive] to fuck it all up at *Glamour*—she's just an inch away. I like reading women's magazines more than I like reading men's."[11]

O, The Oprah Magazine has featured lengthy, informative interviews with former South African president Nelson Mandela and holocaust survivor and author Elie Wiesel. Stories on sex trafficking (*Glamour*); conflicts in Sierra Leone, South Africa, the Middle East, and Northern Ireland, among others *(Marie Claire, Harper's Bazaar,* and *Glamour);* global healthcare issues like addiction to the antidepressant Paxil (*Glamour*), stem-cell research (*Ladies' Home Journal, Good Housekeeping,* and *Vanity Fair*); and stories about women (moms) abusing alcohol and prescription drugs (*Self, O, Glamour* and others) showcase that women's magazines are becoming increasingly adept at covering issues of importance to women worldwide.

In a 2008 Huffington Post article titled "Time to Have a Little Talk about Those Women's Magazines," chick slicks are lauded for the coverage of important issues they have brought forward.[13] The writer remembers a *Glamour* story in which women killed across the country by their intimate partners garnered a multipart article complete with pages of mugshots of the convicted murderers, highlighting deathly domestic abuse like never before. The HuffPo story tells us *Essence* had their own photographer follow Obama on the campaign trail, capturing its own unique images. *Good Housekeeping* did a powerful piece, "You Can't Live Here Unless You're White," on illegal housing discrimination still taking place in 2007. And women's magazines ran numerous "justice journalism" stories including deaths due to the nursing shortage, military women at higher risk of death from the anthrax vaccine, and George W. Bush admitting he didn't know who the Taliban were are all mentioned as leading women's magazine stories on important political issues.

And globally, in a search of ten years worth of the U.K. edition of *Marie Claire*, one researcher found that Muslim women were covered in a whopping 44 percent of the magazines.[14] The author, Arwa Aburawa, found that exactly half the articles portrayed Muslim women as victims, while the other half showed them as independent, empowered women. "In fact, most of the articles followed the typical 'Triumph over Tragedy' trajectory

Readers Respond

"Sometimes, I come across a story in these magazines that makes me want to say, 'Right on, ladies!' Jumping out of all the bullshit beauty and diet tips is a real story about real issues."

—Michelle, communications consultant

popular in women's magazines, which go into painful detail about how women are oppressed and then conclude that, by some miracle, a woman has stepped up to challenge this oppression and will emerge triumphant," said Aburawa.[15]

But no matter what political issues the glossies have focused on, there's no question the depth and breadth of them has continued to evolve. As you saw in the last section, women's mags took their political coverage up a notch during the 2008 election cycle and became even more responsive to the political culture of American women. *Vogue* and *Glamour's* politics were particularly comprehensive, along with several other magazines, including *Working Woman* and *Working Mother*. An August 2011 issue of *Vogue*, for instance, covered Republican presidential candidate Jon Huntsman in an unbiased look at his life, his politics, his family, and his religion and found heady comparisons between Huntsman and Obama (their age, their athletic build, and their wholly unflappable natures) and stark differences between Huntsman and Romney (mainly that Huntsman considers himself a "Jack Mormon," which is a brand of the religion that may not necessarily follow all its strictures). The piece manages to stick to the facts without getting bogged down in any of the rhetoric. Likewise, magazines like *Working Mother* regularly cover top political moms in Washington, D.C.; paid family-leave issues; the state of maternity leave; and profiles of every power-playing woman in politics, regardless of their parties.

Additionally, while women's magazines may not consider themselves "advocacy" publications, per se, they do their part to keep important issues at the forefront, particularly those that are critical to women, like reproductive freedom. Articles on the topic are mainstays in mags like *Glamour* and *Marie Claire,* and not just pieces on abortion but also emergency contraception, birth con-

trol, health insurance, and everything related to women's reproductive health. A May 2006 *Glamour* story, "The New Lies about Women's Health," took a comprehensive look at how local, state, and federal policies (including those of the Bush administration) affected women's healthcare. *Glamour's* coverage was lauded for increasing public awareness of the issue.

Then in 2009, writer Liz Welch won a Maggie (Planned Parenthood award recognizing excellence in media, arts, and entertainment for enhancing the public's understanding of reproductive rights and healthcare) for her article in *Glamour*, "Abortion, the Serious Health Decision Women Aren't Talking about until Now." While the coverage skewed remarkably honest and included women's personal stories of their abortion experiences, the prochoice coverage touted abortion as just another health decision without considering the moral, ethical, or spiritual struggles women might experience in having an abortion. The underlying implication was that every woman—from a nineteen-year-old college student to a forty-five-year-old hockey mom—may one day be faced with what amounted to a simple health choice, like getting a flu shot. While informative and timely, the article nonetheless approached the issue from a very limited and biased perspective.

The nature of reproductive choice has always been a sticky wicket, but the underlying problem, of course, is that a woman's body is the center of politics in the first place. Since magazines are first and foremost about what women want—or what editors believe women want—and are also largely liberal, as are most of the editors, it's a no-brainer that reproductive health would be addressed in a more political way. A February 2012 article in *Glamour,* for example, includes an essay from Oscar-nominated actress Maggie Gyllenhaal, titled, "We Have to Fight for What We Believe In." In it, the actress says an attack on Planned Parenthood is an attack on women's health. Gyllenhaal tells us that over eighty abortion restrictions were enacted in 2011 (wow, talk about overlegislating)—more than double the previous record in 2005, and she reminds us that not only abortion rights, but also funding that provides important screenings for cervical cancer and STDs, preventive care, health exams, and treatments are being slashed in numerous states under the guise of shutting down one resource: Planned Parenthood, the critical provider of healthcare for underserved women, for which 90 percent of services go toward preventive care and 3 percent to abortion care. Gyllenhaal is an effective and engaging spokeswoman for the issue, given not only her name recognition as an actress but also her own story about attending her first Planned Parenthood rally in the sixth-grade with her mother. When magazines feel it's necessary to play their advocacy card, they do it in full force, which makes them political by nature—and naturally biased toward certain outcomes. Of course,

what woman's going to argue with the logic of championing such a vital institution as Planned Parenthood? Oh, yeah. Conservative female politicians—and their constituents. Thus, it's easy to see the sticky place magazines may find themselves when trying to be fair and balanced in their political coverage.

It's no wonder, then, that these types of pieces were the political pulp of the past few years, especially since 2011–2012 saw the House of Representatives's unprecedented assault on women's reproductive rights. Whether they were trying to pass a bill to defund Planned Parenthood or proposing legislation that would allow hospitals who receive federal funds to refuse reproductive care to women even if their life was at stake, over and over conservative legislation was introduced that appeared antagonistic toward women's rights, and pieces like this serve to remind women what it is we're fighting for, and why. And more, the women's magazines are one of the few bastions of prowomen ideals, presenting stories month after month that resonate in important ways with most women, giving us a place to unify under common political sensibilities, if not at the expense of others (like beauty ideals).

The degree to which government is involved in our lives—from regulating business and remediating toxic waste to providing social services and enforcing laws—is truly the core difference between liberal and conservative viewpoints. Women's magazines, liberal by nature because they cater to an audience whose rights have traditionally been sidelined—if not blatantly undermined—by the conservative elect, do try to incorporate balance in their pages, but they're not always successful.

For example, the Consumer Alert / Media Research Center (a conservative watchdog group) analyzed the political policy-oriented coverage that appeared in thirteen women's and family magazines between the months of October 1995 and September 1996. Of the thirteen magazines studied, there were 115 positive portrayals of government activism and/or calls for more government intervention, while there were only eighteen negative portrayals and/or calls for less action.[18]

The study found that *Working Woman* and *Glamour* were the most biased in favor of expanding government, while *Good Housekeeping* was next. *Ladies' Home Journal* was the most politically balanced magazine in the study. During the year studied, the monthly ran ten stories promoting bigger government, it also ran six supporting limited government, and four balanced articles covering both sides of the issues. Interesting here, too, that eight years after this study, Myrna Blyth, longtime former editor-in-chief of *LHJ*, came out with her book *Spin Sisters*, in which she accused the media of its liberal bent and declared that she was a card-carrying right-winger who was uncomfortable with all the "left-leaning" women in her media circles as well as the liberal bent in the glossies and the morning shows.

The issue, according to the Consumer Alert study, was that women's magazines either misled their readers or didn't provide the whole story about the overall impact that "big government" policies or actions have on women and families. For example, articles on contaminated drinking water that were examined in 1995—*Good Housekeeping* (November), *Parents* (March), and *Mademoiselle* (September)—were found to inflate the risks and omit a balanced view. With titles like "Troubled Waters" and "What's in Your Water," they reported an alarmist study about agricultural pesticide runoff contaminating water supplies across the country.

The study also showed that while conservative and/or Republican women were occasionally profiled by the chick slicks, their political views were often challenged instead of celebrated. New Jersey Governor Christine Todd Whitman was profiled for the November 1995 issue of *Working Woman*. While the story was mostly positive, the writer took a potshot at Whitman's tax-cutting policies: "In order to cut income taxes by 30 percent, she has increased long-term borrowing, reduced payments to public pension funds, and cut state aid to local governments. The ripple effect of those steps is yet to be fully realized."[20]

The study also found that Republican women were praised only when working to expand the role of government. Republican senator Nancy Kassebaum, for example, was chosen as one of *Glamour*'s Women of the Year in 1996 for working to ban assault weapons, for expanding regulation of healthcare, and for, not being "extreme." Of the more balanced pieces, according to the

Insider Input

"Funny, isn't it, that women's magazines like *Marie Claire*, *Glamour* and *Redbook* and so many others give you lots of opinions when it comes to prices and styles in their fashion features. . . . But whether in their editorials or between the lines of their feature stories, they offer you only one opinion, about any and all social or political issues."[19]

—Myrna Blyth, former magazine editor and author, *Spin Sisters*

analysis, *Good Housekeeping* devoted the back page of each issue to an essay by former Reagan speechwriter Peggy Noonan. Though Noonan rarely mentioned public policy issues in her essays, this was more of a backhanded nod to balance.

Not much has changed since that study. A 2012 Pew Research Center survey of 1,000 adults reported that 67 percent of Americans see "a great deal" or "fair amount" of political bias in the news media. Too bad, since 68 percent said they prefer to get their political news from sources "that have no particular political point of view."[21]

When *Glamour* names its annual Women of the Year Awards, most of the honorees are liberals in good standing, with a record of lengthy liberal causes under their belts. Winners in 2012 included Withelma Ortiz-Macey (known as "T," former sex trafficking victim now advocating against sex trafficking in this country), Ariana Huffington, Gabrielle Giffords, Esraa Abdel Fattah (also known as the Facebook Girl who live-updated on Facebook from Cairo's Tahrir Square demanding freedom), as well as a host of celebrities, actresses, comedians, and designers: Jennifer Lopez,

Tory Burch, Chelsea Handler, Lea Michele, and Cindy Sherman, with a lifetime achievement award going to Gloria Steinem. The only known conservatives in the bunch: Laura Bush and her daughters, Jenna Bush Hager and Barbara Bush, were honored for their global work advocating for women.

But here again lies the rub: despite their fluff and undermining messaging, women's magazines are still one of the few outlets that are fiercely dedicated to women's issues, which by and large fall far afield of conservative ideals. Thus, it's no wonder magazines like *Glamour* laud the good works of nonconservative women over Tea Party favorites and hard-line Republican ladies. Our lefty lassies are tirelessly pinch-hitting for our rights.

How does all this play out with the readers? Well, how women are influenced and involved politically has been tied to the information they read in the glossies. According to research, women with a sense of autonomy that stems from secure relationships and connections to other women who model what they'd like to become have a greater political understanding. It seems reading about the issues, and especially female politicians, provides us with a yardstick from which to measure ourselves.

Researchers at the University of Toronto and McGill University examined how women acquired political information and how it impacted their voting patterns during the 2000 Canadian election cycle. Interestingly, friendship with other women and their social connections seems to play a role in how women vote. Women with a wide and diverse social network (think loads of personal acquaintances and a significant following on Facebook) tend to vote more liberally. Researchers speculate that the wider the range of women you know and interact with, the more likely you are to vote progressively.[22] The research is important since it implies that reading about political women and their issues in the glossies not only offers us valued information but also a sisterhood community that actually stands in as our social circle. After all, women's magazine's tone and style are that of chatting with a close friend. In this instance, our close friend is often liberal.

But no matter where on the political spectrum you fall, supporting magazines whose political coverage champions women and women's rights, while removing the sexist undertones from women candidates, will continue to promote positive political coverage for women, no matter if that coverage appears liberal, conservative, unbiased, or fluffy. As with all editorial content in women's magazines, it's up to us, the readers, to use a discerning eye when evaluating political coverage and to insist that our favorite glossies present well-rounded political coverage.

Chapter 9

THE BIG O

A dress makes no sense unless it inspires men to want to take it off you.
—Anna Wintour

Pick up almost any women's magazine on the stands today and there's at least one article about sex. In a magazine like *Cosmo*, nearly equivalent to *Playgirl* in content these days, it's more like a half dozen.

Unfortunately, the chick slicks aren't always in touch with what's going down between our sheets when it comes to sex and relationships, but you wouldn't know it from advice columns, expert sources, and "reader" anecdotes that purport to know otherwise. We are told what to wear, how to act, and what to say, not only in the bedroom but also outside of it. We're schooled on how to find and keep a man, how to blow his mind in bed, how to act around his friends, and when to suggest everything from shacking up to marriage to kids. We are told how to get our way, win a fight, negotiate a truce, and when to give in. It's a collective primer, rehashed each month, on how to conform to narrow ideals of female sexuality and gender roles.

But what if you don't conform to gender stereotypes or want to dress provocatively or slather yourself in chocolate syrup or leave hints about the ring you desire? And what would you think if you knew your boyfriend or husband were taking men's magazine advice on how to get *his* way, delay commitment, finagle a threesome or that chocolate syrup thing, or how to skimp on the ring but make you love it anyway? A bit sexist, eh? Now consider *this* alternative: What if *you* wanted to delay commitment, have a threesome, split the chores equally, be the breadwinner, or enjoy an egalitarian relationship with a man—or even another woman—without having to squelch your own desires, independence, and sexual identity? Pretty liberating. Unfortunately, these are not ideals that get much play in the glossy pages of our magazines. Instead, women's magazines tend to limit female sexuality to traditional heterosexual stereotypes, right down to the sex-play tips that rarely stray beyond predictable boundaries.

Insider Input

"As an older woman and a spokesperson for ageless sexuality, I find that my age group is largely invisible in the women's magazines' treatment of sexuality. The only exception is when they notice the gorgeous sex appeal of an older celebrity, like Helen Mirren. But celebrate the sexuality of the rest of us older women, or offer us sexual self-help? No, that's only for those without wrinkles—or life experience!"

—Joan Price, author of *Naked at Our Age: Talking Out Loud about Senior Sex* and *Better Than I Ever Expected: Straight Talk about Sex After Sixty*

In her 2001 study of *Cosmopolitan* and *Playboy* magazines, Nicole Krassas, PhD, an assistant professor of political science and women's studies at Eastern Connecticut State University, found that women's magazines contain a single vision of female sexuality—that "women should primarily concern themselves with attracting and sexually satisfying men."[1]

The study showed that both men and women received the same messages about sexuality in two very different magazines, one aimed at men, the other women. The message: women are sexual objects and men view women as sexual objects.

GLOSSY FACT

A 1998 study in the *Journal of Sex Research* found that *Seventeen* magazine doubled the number of sexual stories they ran from 1974 to 1994, including articles on a wide variety of sexual topics, such as recreational sex. Other research showed that stories simultaneously encouraged girls to be sexually alluring while reminding them to be chaste.[2]

When it comes to women's magazines overall, however, the blame does not rest squarely on *Cosmo's* provocative shoulders. Nearly every glossy covers some aspect of sex from behind this narrow lens, albeit some more responsibly than others. Whether it's the subtleties of improving marital sex in magazines like *Redbook,* or the more blatant pieces in *Women's Health* or *Glamour,* with titles like "How to Turn Him on Again" and "The Top 25 Moves to Blow His Mind in Minutes," the content shares a common message: Learn How to Please Your Man Before It's Too Late.

It doesn't help that there is an abundance of mixed messages as well: be coy and flirtatious to win his affections, but once you do, be hyperfocused on keeping your sexual dynamics titillating to avoid losing him, even at the expense of your own sensibilities and pleasure.

Fortunately, while yes, content hews pretty tightly to the dynamics of traditional heterosexual relationships between young attractive people, a shared redeeming quality among them is that in spite of the dredge and the dreck, the sensational and ridiculous, women's magazines have consistently included news, insight, stories, and information about women's sexual health, reproductive rights, family planning, STDs, cancer prevention and care, and sensitive topics like rape, abuse, and sexual dysfunction. And occasionally, between the quick and dirty "sex surveys," skewed facts, and trumped up "expert advice," content appears that surprises with its progressive prowoman take on sexual freedom and empowerment. This is why we keep coming back to these magazines, despite their failings.

IT'S A MAN'S WORLD . . . OR IS IT?

One problem with sex articles in the women's magazines is that they seem to lose sight of the fact that it is the woman who should be the focus here. Unfortunately, much of the content still surrounds the lone conviction that women need to know how to get a man, keep a man happy, please a man in bed, and prevent the loss of the relationship with a man. And if you do lose the man, here's how to do it all over again next time.

Here's a prime example of an article that focuses on how you can satisfy your guy's sexual proclivities: "Kinky Lite, Sex Moves Guys Love." Since it appears in the January 2012 *Cosmo,* it's naturally treated more provocatively. The feature covers a spectrum of "kinky" acts—from ordering him not to get an erection when you go down on him to tying his hands to the headboard with his tie, and it comes complete with two sidebar symbol boxes for how kinky *he* thinks it is, from mild to freaky; and how often *he* wants to do it, from never to all the time. Interestingly, the one "freaky" suggestion that is actually *empowering* to women—hand him your vibrator and tell him to use it on himself while you watch—is not

Insider Input

"These types of articles teach women that sex isn't about us or for us. Instead, it's all about satisfying (or failing to satisfy) other people's agendas for our body. It's almost impossible to avoid absorbing that idea to some extent, if you're a woman. And the consequences are serious: not only do we feel alienated from our bodies, not only do we feel like we're failing all the time as women (because not one of us can live up to all those contradictory ideals), not only do we miss out on the pleasure and satisfaction that can come from exploring our sexuality on our own terms, but when we're systematically alienated from our own desires, needs, and boundaries. . . . It can also leave us very vulnerable to people who want to do harm to us, or to manipulate us to their own ends."

—Jaclyn Friedman, author of *What You Really Want: The Smart Girl's Shame-Free Guide to Sex and Safety* surprisingly also one of the only tips that earns a "never "in the how often he wants to do it rating. What else is off-kilter in this piece? We women were not asked to rate each of these acts. It's simply assumed we'll accommodate our man's preferences, regardless of where the act falls on *our* spectrum of "never to all the time."

As luck would have it, this same issue contains excellent info in the Gyno Health Report, a regular column that's combo Q&A and FYI of small tidbits of sexual health info such as, "why is my vagina ultrasensitive after orgasm?" and "if my guys' penis is red and flakey, could this be an STD?" If more of *Cosmo's* content contained interesting or useful sexual health and wellness information for young women readers with legit sexual health or even sexual behavior or relationship answers—rather than the how-to-please-your-man staples—*Cosmo* could be of much more value to young women. Too often, however, the sex stories are followed by relationship articles in the same mancentric manner that play upon gender stereotypes and women's insecurities, like why your man is a commitment-phobe and how you can slyly bring him around to marriage and kids.

Krassas' research reveals that pieces like these tell us how we should look and how we should act in order to attain sexual satisfaction and satisfy our man. They tell us how important sex is to our lives, and they "promote the idea that women should primarily concern themselves with attracting and sexually satisfying men."[3]

And in that same how to please your man vein, there's the February 2012 *Glamour* piece titled "Guy Pretty vs. Girl Pretty," which discusses the subjective difference between what guys think is attractive on women and what women think is attractive. For instance, guys like a natural lip whereas women like red lipstick, and guys like a little mascara whereas women like shadow, liner, and a done-up eye like the smoky eye treatment every women's mag shows you how to pull off on a monthly basis. Women apparently like short hair, but guys love it long. All of this to imply that women should just dump the lipstick, the eye shadow, and the short hair in favor of what guys want, or in this case, some archaic version of what *Glamour* says guys want since they also include things about how guys are creeped out by eyelash curlers, all manners of hair removal and giant hair bows.[4] (Who the hell wears giant hair bows anymore?)

Of course, occasionally, sex content empowers women readers by providing the kinds of story angles that help women redefine their sexuality and play into the types of prowoman topics we want more of. Sometimes, the magazines—even the worst offenders among them—get it right, even if the topics are a bit over the top or intentionally titillating.

The January 2011 issue of *Cosmo,* for example, includes a feature titled, "Meet Your Other G-Spot!" The article, which is all about the pleasure that comes from nipple stimulation, goes into great depth about the hows and whys of nipple-induced orgasms. It cites research showing that sensations from the nipples travel to the same part of the brain as sensations from the vagina, clitoris, and cervix do.

At three pages, it stands out as one of that month's biggest features. Broken into three parts, from beginner to intermediate to advanced, it tackles "nip action," as the writer likes to call it, and outlines just how your partner should stimulate your nipples to help you achieve orgasm.

In a sympathetic turn, the article reassures women that it's okay if you're not nipple-sensitive. Not all bodies are created equal. If a nipple-induced big-O isn't possible for you, no biggie, but if it is, fantastic! It's one of those rare pieces focusing exclusively on the woman's pleasure, which is refreshing, even inspiring. Similarly, the October 2011 *Women's Health* ran a feature titled "Your New To-Do-It List: Being a Bit More Brazen in Bed Can Be the Ultimate Way to Boost Your Satisfaction." Yay to *WH* for actually caring about *us* getting *ours!* The article encourages women to slip out of their comfort zone and try some new sex stuff—solely for our enjoyment. On the sexual to-dos were items like sext someone, use food play, read the *Kama Sutra,* or have your partner dress up.

STRAIGHT TALK

Not all magazine content is as overt as *Cosmo's* in perpetuating the narrow, one-size-fits-all ideal of female sexuality as distinctly heterosexual and vanilla. Others appear to be prowoman, but they nonetheless perpetuate traditional stereotypes of sex and relationships. In the January 2012 issue of *Redbook,* for example, a piece titled "The Best Love Advice. Period" couches sex within a love/relationship article that presumes to know the "best" ways for women to keep their marriage enlivened, happy, and healthy, yet in the real world, the range of a woman's sensual triggers, cultural tastes, and emotional needs is as varied as each woman. The

Readers Respond

"When I was single, I read the sex articles more closely and usually wound up feeling incompetent or unusual. Now that I'm happily married, I usually either skip them, or read them with a huge grain of salt."
—Anne, marketing consultant

article offers a "best of" list, including the best time of day for "amazing sex," the best movies about relationships, the best lingerie, the best mattress, the best two things to keep in your bedside table—which of course is the standard lube and a vibrator—the best shade to paint your bedroom, and the best sexy playlist. By their standards your best chance of enlivening your marriage is to watch *The Notebook* wearing a short, sexy nightie with matching panties (nothing too confusing to remove), in a room painted a lovely shade of Neptune's Home; then turn on Al Green's "Let's Stay Together" and have sex on a mattress where you both can choose how firm or soft your side should be, like with a Sleep Number mattress, at six in the morning. (Oh, and don't forget the standard-size vibrator if you really want to spice things up!)

But what if you fall outside this incredibly tight stereotype of "normal" female sexual experience? What if you're—gasp!—gay? The messaging is anything but empowering. It's alienating.

Take Laura Laing, author of *Math for Grownups*. She explains that when she was a tween, she was obsessed with reading *Teen* and *Seventeen* magazines. "My mother wouldn't let me buy them until I was an actual teenager, and so on my thirteenth birthday, I walked through a blizzard to purchase my first copy of *Teen* from the local IGA. At the time, I had no idea I was a lesbian. Growing up in a small town, I was blissfully assuming that I would marry a man and live happily ever after."

By the time Laing graduated from college, her life looked a lot different. "I had come out and was in a relationship with my current partner. Unlike most twentysomethings, I simply didn't consider picking up *Cosmo* or *Marie Claire*. Not only could I not relate to the stories—"Make Your Man Happy in Bed"—but the decidedly antifeminist bent to most of the content was off-putting. In short, I couldn't see myself in the pages."

Nor can any woman who doesn't conform to the hetero-sexual ideal.

What about women who are bisexual, or who like to domi-nate or initiate sex? Again, they're largely absent from these gloss-ies. As are women who've shown a sexual fluidity in which their sexual preferences and desires shift with age. These women won't find themselves on the pages of the glossies either.

Noted sexual researcher Alfred Kinsey, along with his col-leagues, developed the "Kinsey Scale" back in 1948, which showed that people did not fit into rigid heterosexual or homosexual cat-egories. In *Sexual Behavior of the Human Female*, Kinsey writes, "Sex-ual behavior is either normal or abnormal, socially acceptable or unacceptable, heterosexual or homosexual; and many persons do not want to believe that there are gradations in these matters from one to the other extreme."[5]

In fact, a 2011 study by the Williams Institute of the UCLA School of Law found that 4 percent of the American population (or around ten million people) identifies as gay, lesbian, bisexual, and transgender.[6] Unfortunately these groups aren't represented in the perfumed pages of the chick slicks either.

What's more, a 2011 study from Boise State University pub-lished in the *Journal of Sex Research* found that 60 percent of women surveyed had bisexual feelings that increased with age. Forty-five percent had kissed a woman, and 50 percent of respondents had fantasized about it.[7]

And while it's tempting to chalk up this blatant blind eye to the old adage "write what you know," some editors are actually knowingly perpetuating the schism between the narrow ideals printed in the glossies and the reality that there's a rich spectrum of female sexuality outside the pages. For example, I wrote a sexual health article for one of the women's magazines and mentioned that woman-on-woman sex had a somewhat lowered risk of certain STDs. In the pitch, the health editor wanted to know all about this, but when the final copy was approved by the editor-in-chief, all mention of lesbian sex was removed with the comment that "we don't have enough gay readers to include this."

Perhaps if they started including more diverse content, they *would*.

ARE MAGAZINES "FAKING IT"?

Universal stories about sex are presented as journalism, bursting with conjecture and woman-on-the-street quotes, and they are taken at face value by many readers. From the surveys to the experts to the lack of fact-checking, skewed data, or manufactured quotes, sadly they're a demoralizing cultural phenomenon, shaping and reinforcing what women believe about men, sexual practices, orgasms, and relationships. Women's magazines run carefully reported and fact-checked articles on subjects such as heart disease and retirement planning, yet some writers, editors, and fact-checkers involved in sex articles admit the editorial standards for them are seriously lacking.

Laurie Abraham, executive editor of *Elle* at the time she spoke at a Mediabistro panel, "The Pink Ghetto? Why Women's Magazines Get No Respect," explained that working with composite characters enable editors to alter quotes to suit their stories. She told the panel about writing a relationship article for a women's magazine and how a quote from one of her sources about the number of times she had sex was changed because it didn't jive with the editor's perception. "This happens to any magazine that deals in these relationship stories, which involve interviewing a lot of people. They always do composites; they always take out information that is disconcerting. And that's the way it works."[8]

Seems sex stories may not come with as scrupulous a journalistic bent as other articles. Within professional circles I move there have long been reports that names are changed much more frequently surrounding sex articles, ages are altered to fit within the magazine's demographic, and writers and editors often interview friends and family for sexual anecdotes, which is taboo in most other types of journalism. And who's to say sex stories aren't wildly mad-libbed? Just as articles are fashioned and constructed to fit the ideal by the editors and writers, sex pieces are notorious for being shoehorned into a box—a one-size-fits-all heterosexual formula wherein each piece of the sexy puzzle is plastered into place to make up the whole story. Did Marta S. from Minnesota *really* get busy under the blanket on a redeye flight to France in a piece that asks women what their most unusual location for sex was, or did Chrissy T. think that her black swan costume from last Halloween spiced up her love life in an article about breaking out of a boring sex routine? These "sexadotes" (sexual anecdotes) are ripe for skepticism; they may or may not be complete fabrications to fit a storyline, depending on what the editors want to run in that issue.

Which brings us to the question of sex surveys in the women's magazines. These are what are called quick-and-dirty surveys where the magazine emails or phones up a certain amount of people, say three hundred men, and compiles results and summarizes the research. While they suggest a scientific approach, they aren't in-depth scientific surveys or studies in which other published data are looked at and taken into consideration. They often don't tell you the questions asked, and ethical policies like making sure the questions are understandable or not misinterpreted aren't even taken into consideration. The surveys are unscientific and often send mixed messages, skewed to fit the magazine's needs.

Dr. Petra Boynton, a U.K. psychologist and sex and relationship expert, says, "A really good piece of sex research takes ages to put together because you go and look for existing research. In magazine surveys, they never look at existing research."[9] Boynton says that instead, a group of editors sit around an office and come up with the questions, always with their angle and headlines in mind. Another clue that something is amiss is that they don't include the question(s) originally asked for the magazine surveys—only the results. She also says to beware of the mixed messaging magazine surveys may send. One *Cosmo* survey she reviewed found that a large number of women (70 percent) were insecure about what they looked like during sex, yet the same survey included that 60 percent of women thought they were good in bed. That's sort of contradictory.

Boynton also explains that women's mags walk a fine line between being naughty and nice in their sex content while trying to hang on to advertisers. "They focus on heterosexual sex, monogamy, straight couples having sex within fairly safe and predictable ways." For instance, a threesome, if mentioned, would always include a guy and two girls (the latter doing the interacting), never two girls doing something to a guy, as that might be perceived as too risqué. The same with anal sex—if it's written about at all—it's a guy doing it to a woman, it's never going to be two women or a woman doing it to a guy.[10]

In the February 2012 issue of *Redbook,* a tongue-in-cheek quiz asks readers, "What is your Real Age . . . In Bed?" The cutesy quiz, half joke, half reality for married working moms (*Redbook's* demographic), focuses on how often you're doing it or not, how long—or short—it lasts, the most unusual place you've had sex, and how your physical flexibility is holding up, assigning you, based on your answers, an age of 19, 39, or 69 in bed. This is yet another example of the insidious way in which content undermines a woman's sense of sexual confidence. If you're 30 and rate a 69 in bed, is that an empowering feeling? Likely not.

Insider Input

Laurie Abraham, at the time executive editor of *Elle* magazine, warns that the biggest problem with women's magazines is how much fibbing surrounds sex content. "The fundamental issue is how we lie about sex and how we lie about how women live. I mean, I do feel we engage in a certain amount of lying."[11]

When it comes to using "expert" sources in articles about sex, there's also a level of credibility under question. For instance, in the January/February 2012 issue of *Women's Health,* a male writer sets out to prove that women want "dirty talk" in a piece dubbed "The Art of Aural Sex: A Brave Male Writer Signs Up for a Serious Lesson in Dirty Talk." The gist of the article is that essentially guys love women to talk dirty during sex, but though women crave it too, guys are afraid they'll get it wrong so they often refrain. The piece comments that some great dirty talk could send a woman teetering on the brink of orgasm for twenty minutes if only they could learn the nasty language of love. Though it's doubtful most women's pleasure hinges on men's erotic vocab, the brave writer sets out to learn how. Problem is, the expert in the piece gives advice that's more awkward than arousing, suggesting this winning line: "I want to disrobe you and see your parts exposed and touch them . . ."

Really? That's the advice from the sexpert? That's the hot phrase that will get every woman on the planet fired up below the belt? In fairness to the writer, even he realizes the cheese factor and claims he has several exes that would run screaming from the bed if he ever delivered that one-liner. But the sex therapist expert (and author of a book on sex) just further educates him about what to do when and if the dirty talk backfires, saying, "Come here and give me a hug. I hope I didn't offend you—are you okay?"

This problem stems more with the expert used, which readers rarely take into consideration. Boynton warns that an expert, say funded by a drug company that produces a sexual dysfunction medication, would not be the go-to source for a piece on a couple's sexual problems, yet it's this type of expert placement often seen.[12] Beware, too, she says, of experts who want to sell you something, ones who tout only one treatment for an issue (such as surgery, medication, or a home remedy), or those who just give "lame" advice. Editors walk a tightrope of advertising placement and subtle source issues, especially within sex articles, but you never want your expert as the go-to source in a sex article selling you something.

Insider Input

"Frankly, I think the really good journalists get frustrated writing for women's magazines. Why should they spend their life writing 'Seven Tips for Greater Sex?' It may be something you do sometimes to pay the bills or something, and it may have its certain payoffs—maybe you learn something, right? But I mean, come on, this cannot be the height of someone's journalistic career."[13]
—Chandra Czape, former deputy articles editor, *Cosmopolitan*

SEEKING THE RIGHT TOUCH

Yet for all that the magazines do wrong when it comes to sex, there is still a lot of good in some of the content. The chick slicks deliver important news and information about female sexual health, and occasionally, sex itself. Sometimes, the glossies succeed at presenting balanced, fact-based pieces on everything from reproductive choice, and the pros/cons of different types of birth control methods (a topic I've written about many times over the years for several different mags), but also of STDs, family planning, sexual dysfunction, sexual empowerment, illnesses unique to women (such as ovarian, cervical, uterine, and breast cancer;

polycystic ovarian syndrome, endometriosis, PMS, and others). They have also educated countless women, young and old, on important issues unique to our vajayjays, minus an agenda other than awareness. Sexuality pieces even debunk myths from time to time and teach women not only that their sexual fulfillment matters, but also that they must seek the kind of sex and sexual partner that is right for them, a mantra magazines like *Ms.* began promoting from the beginning.

For instance, the June 2012 issue of *Marie Claire* ran small stories on what faking your orgasm might mean for your relationship, how online dating is getting safer (major sites recently agreed to do background checks to screen for sex offenders), and how the scent of your man greatly influences your relationship. The June 2012 *Women's Health* included "The Secrets to Having a Stronger Finish," a four-page spread on achieving bigger and better orgasms. And the June 2012 *Self* ran a playful but interesting piece on how each week of your menstrual cycle measures up with your sex drive, called "The Best Nights for Hot Sex." While it was humorous and tongue-in-cheek, it was supported by medical research and studies that clearly show how physiological differences in mood and hormone levels can and do realistically affect a woman's sex drive. Across the board on a good month, you'll find similar topics when it comes to sex. Some miss the mark, yes, but others provide a wealth of sexual information for women who wouldn't be the wiser without these glossy magazines.

There's no question sex in the women's magazines walks a fine line between the raunchier the better (*Cosmo*) and a straight and narrow streamlined idea of what's normal and not too freakish (*Redbook*). While *Cosmo* historically exaggerates to the twelfth degree to make copy as scintillating and arousing as possible, pubs like *Redbook* wobble somewhere this side of prude, running nothing too deviant or disdainful. Mags like *Self, Marie Claire, Women's Health,* and *Glamour* jump on the sex wagon each month, falling somewhere midstream of the two fringes, and deliver something between helpful, informational content and hyped up, provocative fluff. The majority of the Six Sisters refrain from blatant sex pieces, though they occasionally provide mild crossover content in articles about relationships, marriage, dating, or sexual health. Editors also must walk a fine advertorial line, since if content dials up the raunch factor, advertisers may bolt (although clearly, *Cosmo's* advertisers have a higher threshold for lascivious content). For this reason, most articles are sexually vanilla in the women's mags with regard to hetero sex, and monogamous relationships, though mileage may vary.

There's no question sex sells, and the photos inside, often retouched and digitally remastered to perfection, continue to convey what the women's magazines think is sexy. Again, this ideal is preset for you and is as difficult to live up to as the magazine's unreal standard of beauty.

*   *   *

Although women's sexuality is no longer taboo in most of the women's magazines, researchers continue to debate whether the shameless sexualization of women's bodies within these magazines is liberating or further degrading. Plus, putting out a generation of women schooled only in the sex advice from the glossies may not only set feminism back sixty years but may just put these very same women at a huge disadvantage as they define their own sexual identities. Going forward, we can only hope that calling out women's magazines on squeezing women readers into a one-size-fits-all sexual ideal via blog posts, Twitter storms, Facebook postings, and continued media scrutiny, will make magazines more accountable for the sexual content they publish.

Chapter 10

CELEBRITY CENTRAL

Never ask anyone what kind of tree they want to be.
—Barbara Walters

From *Vogue* to *Vanity Fair,* and *Redbook* to *Self,* a celebrity on the cover of a women's glossy sells copies. Plain and simple. This wasn't always the case. Far from it, in fact. To understand how this ubiquitous practice came into being, we first have to go back several decades to understand where said celebrity coverage even came from.

It was likely birthed back in 1974 when *People,* the brainchild of Time, Inc., arrived on the newsstands. The first issue with Mia Farrow, the star of the movie *The Great Gatsby,* graced the cover. It sold more than a million copies—unheard of for a startup publication. During its glory days in the 1970s and 80s, it inspired a new niche of magazines that focused on celebrities, from best-selling authors and top models, actors, and actresses, to sports figures who had risen to fame. It was the birth of a reporting phenomenon: personality journalism. Readers wanted to see, learn, and know about famous people—and they still do today.

In 1991, the editor-in-chief of *Vogue*, Anna Wintour, perhaps playing off *People's* widespread success, put Kim Basinger on the cover and presented her in a fashion layout fit for royalty, followed in short succession by the likes of Winona Ryder and Sharon Stone. Suddenly, actresses were modeling clothing and magazine sales soared.

GLOSSY FACT

Women's magazines that don't use celebrities on the cover: *Woman's Day, Family Circle, Real Simple,* and *Southern Living.*

In 1992, *InStyle* got smart to the idea of celebrity covers rather than the models they normally splashed on the front of their magazine. Surprise, surprise! Actresses could popularize, glamorize, and sell us fashion—and hence, fashion magazines—even more effectively than the supermodels assigned to this task. This small, slow step of evolution not only helped make *InStyle* a leading fashion magazine, but it also spilled onto the glossy fronts of other women's magazines so that by the midnineties, women's magazines had transitioned from covers with supermodels like Naomi Campbell, Cindy Crawford, Kate Moss, and Claudia Schiffer to the actresses of the day: Demi Moore, Julia Roberts, and Meryl Streep.

DEATH OF THE DIVA, RISE OF THE STAR

While the occasional fashion magazine like *Vogue* or *Harper's Bazaar* still runs a rare model on the cover, today the only models able to land said cover are those who've crossed over to celebrityville: Gisele Bundchen, Tyra Banks, and Heidi Klum, to name a few—models who've become renowned for more than just modeling, who design clothing, act, or host television shows, for instance, and who have morphed beyond modeling into recognizable celebrities themselves.

By the late 1990s, the tide had totally turned against supermodels as glossy cover girls. One catalyst is said to be changes in the fashion trends, which moved away from glam and toward grunge, hip-hop, and post-punk street style, which was largely dictated by popular music of the time. These larger-than-life supermodels, who were pivotal parts of both runway shows and magazine covers, had a level of glitz, polish, and personality that didn't gel with the dark, drab, dressed-down styles of the era. Plus, designers wanted their clothing to be the star of the show, whether that was the runway or the magazine photo spread, and supermodels who had developed celebrity personalities redirected the focus away from the clothes. Another theory—one shared in private circles, offices, and cubicles of glossy mags and design houses—was that the demanding behavior of some of the

GLOSSY FACT

Linda Evangelista reportedly was quoted saying, "We (supermodels) don't wake up for less than $10,000 a day," and Naomi Campbell had several run-ins with authorities after hurling cell phones at an assistant and a housekeeper in separate incidents, and causing a ruckus on an airplane when one of her bags went missing.[1]

top-earning supermodels exhausted both magazine editors and designers. Colleagues in the know talked in hushed tones among themselves about the change and jumped on the numerous opportunities to now interview the replacements: celebrities. The Diva was falling out of fashion, literally.

As the careers of the big six supermodels of the time (Naomi Campbell, Christy Turlington, Linda Evangelista, Claudia Schiffer, Cindy Crawford, and Kate Moss) ran their course naturally, no other models were primed as replacements. Today, the current crop of models are a thin, young, bunch of beautiful but anonymous faces, said to be kept that way by the design of the most powerful fashion houses and magazine editors in the business.[2]

Insider Input

"The supermodel is dead," Claudia Schiffer told the *Mail* in 2007. "These days, singers and actresses are as likely to grace the covers of glossy magazines, preventing models from reaching star status. . . . Supermodels like we once were don't exist anymore."[3]

Of course, the bottom line is always profit—to find the sweet spot that drives sales and avoid the moves that turn sales sluggish. When magazines discovered that putting the next hot celeb on the cover can crank newsstand sales when subscription and ad pages are falling, it was a no-brainer. Seems subscription sales are often staid throughout the year, but the presence of a hot celeb on a magazine's cover inspires readers to buy the magazine off the rack. In fact, compared to subscription deals, off-the-rack sales are an ever-shifting trend for magazines. A woman who wouldn't think of subscribing to *Vogue*, but who adores Adele, for instance, may pick it up off the stands if she's on the cover, or a woman who is ga-ga for Gwyneth Paltrow but wouldn't necessarily subscribe to *Ladies' Home Journal* may buy that month's issue just to get their Gwynny fix.

Magazines even track their sales in terms of celeb covers. For instance, according to *Adweek,* the top-selling celebs for 2010 mag sales included the number one Sandra Bullock, with stories of her romantic betrayal and newly adopted baby; Angelina Jolie, a perennial favorite for her Brangelina family saga; Lady GaGa, who epitomized musical and personal success that year; the Kardashian sisters, whose reality brand had begun to go viral; and Jennifer Aniston, another recurrent favorite as the beautiful but jilted girl next door, living in the shadow of Brangelina.[4]

For 2011, Jennifer Aniston, Heidi Klum, and Sarah Jessica Parker were the top newsstand-sellers. According to *New York Fashion,* Sarah Jessica Parker's *Elle*, *Vogue*, and *Marie Claire* covers were the second or third bestsellers for each magazine, and Heidi Klum's *Lucky* and *Glamour* covers were both magazines' second best performers that year, while Aniston gave *Marie Claire* its top selling issue in July and brought boosted sales for the November *Elle*.[5] These sale stats are tracked judiciously by magazine marketers, and unfortunately, it's inferred that big sales, or lack thereof, come down to the celebrity. A dud celeb with low magazine sales will not likely be asked back by the magazine anytime soon.

So how did women's magazines come to put celebrities on their covers anyway? It's anybody's guess why it took so long for the likes of *Vogue* or *InStyle* to replicate the success of *People* back in 1974. But after those first few celeb covers sent sales of women's magazines soaring, the celebrity cover zeitgeist was born. And the

interview and/or fashion spread accompanying that celebrity became the centerpiece of the magazine. Now, whether or not that celebrity will send us readers to the magazine racks in droves is the trickier question, with plenty of margin for error.

CELEBRITY WORSHIP SYNDROME

Obviously, we often pick up magazines to *read* about a celebrity who graces the cover, not just ogle their beauty shots. But the two go hand in hand. We're drawn by the promise of "revelations" and the fantasy factor of stylized photo spreads, which allow us to indulge in the idea that celebs are royalty—gifted and glorious in a way we aren't. The photos and content offer a snapshot into a privileged world that fascinates us, and the more intimate details we know about a celeb, the more we're drawn to them and can envision ourselves as their best gal-pal. And apparently, even celebs do this with people *they* admire. On a February 2012 episode of the Ellen DeGeneres Show, for instance, actress Reese Wither-spoon admitted to being smitten with the princess of Wales, Kate Middleton, upon meeting her. Reese poked fun at her own doe-eyed, wide smile expressions in photos with the princess and told Ellen she was hoping Kate would call her and they could become besties. And so it is with readers of the celebrity profile. So much so, that it's an actual "syndrome." In 2003, *The New Scientist* reported that one-third of Americans suffered from CWS (Celebrity Worship Syndrome). Yet why do we care about the personal lives of people we've never met? Social psychologists think the reasons are complex, including boredom, and living vicariously through movie stars as a way of alleviating that boredom. Another reason involves a search for identity, since teenagers score highest on celebrity worship scales. What's more, celebrities conjure fantasy, and fantasy relationships are easier to form than real ones, making celeb reading ripe for the masses.[7]

The hook that reels us in is the expectation of the "revelation," the small inside disclosure or buzz you hope to glean reading the celeb interview. When a magazine interview gives the juice on a celebrity, getting them to admit some little-known truth, some detail about their life that would fascinate readers, some admission of a quirk or a habit or, hell, anything at all that we haven't been privy to prior (won't Jennifer Aniston finally confirm she's in love again or having a baby?), it fosters kinship for the reader, and that translates to associated loyalty to the magazine. But don't be fooled. The "disclosures" that hook a reader are usually quite calculated. Celebrities, their publicist, the interviewer, and the magazine editors generally work in unison to come up with the juicy details that will help sell the interview to the public.

If a magazine dares print something unbecoming, it could piss off the celeb and the publicist, undermining their chances of being granted future interviews. No women's glossies can afford to alienate their bread and butter that way. As a result, most celeb profiles tow a fine line between true disclosure of anything juicy, and the canned fluff about what the celeb does for fun, their eating habits, and a nod to their current romantic entanglement. Of course, this can often translate as mind-numbingly boring. To avoid this, the best profiles dare to disclose some unexpected tidbit, infuse it with humor or pathos, or provide a point by which we identify with the celebrity, like how she walks her dog every morning just the way we do. Perhaps that's where the problems lie with celebrity interviews in the women's glossies.

THE CELEBRITY INTERVIEW BREAKDOWN

If you think spotting Kate Hudson on the cover of your favorite women's glossy at the grocery when you're about to head to her new movie opening this weekend is pure coincidence, don't be naive. Kate or any A-lister's appearance on the cover of a woman's magazine is a carefully orchestrated plan that took place six to eight months prior. Editors compete with each other month after month to score the celeb du jour for their cover. Having the right celebrity at the right month (say, Ms. Hudson when her movie is about to open) is a coup that can up newsstand sales by thousands of copies. Entertainment or booking editors spend large portions of their day schmoozing and wooing celebrity publicists in pursuit of landing the celeb interview, and negotiation is the key to winning.

GLOSSY FACT

In the February 2012 issue of *Social Psychological and Personality Science,* researchers found when women feel a personal connection to a thin celebrity, they're more likely to associate with their similarities than to find differences. Despite many previous findings about women being negatively influenced by thin images in the glossies, seeing a favorite slim star in a magazine may actually give women's self-image a boost.[8] Seems if magazines strive to choose slim celebs that are highly admired, they can minimize the jolt to self-esteem often associated with viewing thin, young models or starlets.

Back when women's magazines simply used models for the covers, whether a celebrity was an A, B, C, or D-list star was of little consequence, but now that virtually every women's magazine uses actresses as cover girls, the caliber of celebrity is crucial. Face recognition equals sales. And it seems every magazine with twelve issues to put out wants the same twelve women on their covers. Think Julia Roberts and Gwyneth Paltrow. Occasionally, a B-list celeb can make the grade if they're having an uptick in popularity, a well-received movie, or some personal drama that usurps their star status, but even this is a risk-taking proposition for the magazine. Editors rarely take calculated risks on bringing in sales with a less bankable celebrity. However, the move scores big points with publicists because if a magazine ran Maggie Gyllenhaal, say, instead of Sandra Bullock, the publicist is said to be so happy to have the publicity for the quirkier, less-moneyed star that they're likely to return the favor by offering up an A-list celebrity from the clientele list at the next interview opportunity.

Yet putting a celeb's face on the cover of a women's mag is a purely money-driven decision. In fact, it may not have much to do with the magazine's readership at all. If the female A-list celeb is in the magazine's demographic and in a new movie or other project during the month's issue, it's a no-brainer. Women's mags only want A-listers, especially for cover stories, since they're proven bestsellers on the stands.

Celebs are all but guaranteed their coverage will be positive and they will come up smelling like daisies. Yes, that means softball questions. The star's PR person then approves everything, from the shoot location to the photographer, makeup artist, hairstylist, and clothes. Even the interviewer may be negotiated in advance. Most writers enjoy working with celebrities. It's their gatekeepers and representatives that play hardball. Yet, publicists work hard for every dollar they earn by often having to manage erratic, egotistical, or difficult celebrity personalities.

Once the glossy's booking or entertainment editor and the celebrity's publicist touch base about an interview, the negotiations begin. Betsy Model, a prominent journalist and celebrity interviewer, says that her long-standing relationship with both editors and publicists and her ability to land big-name interviewees gives her much more leeway when it comes to interview restrictions. Her reputation precedes her, and instead of getting twenty minutes with a celeb where a publicist sits in, she has the opposite experience. She often scores hours, if not days, with the likes of Antonio Banderas or Wynonna Judd sans chaperone, without relinquishing a preview of her questions. Though she clearly admits she is the exception to the rule, with four hundred celebrity profiles to her credit.

Yet because women's magazines are utterly dependent on the celebrity interview, editors agree to a large portion of a publicist's requests and requirements. One editor was quoted in the *Journal of Magazine and New Media Research,* saying, "The problem is . . . because so many deals are made these days and we are all competing for the same celebrities, it's like what are you willing to trade? Photo approval? Copy approval? Writer approval? Because everybody does trade on that, you're seeing stories on celebrities that are not necessarily the real story, just the negotiated story."[9]

Insider Input

"I had a client who owned a security company who has developed an exciting new security product, and I could not let the press have his photo, as he is a private investigator. But editors met that request. One even suggested she might have her art department draw a Sherlock Holmes sketch with cap and pipe!"
—Maire Peters, entertainment publicist

When points can't be negotiated, however, it's not unusual for the entire arrangement to break down and be scrapped. One Tom Cruise/*Rolling Stone* interview referenced in the *Journal of Magazine and New Media Research* study reported that the interview came with one stipulation: the writer could not ask Cruise a single personal question. If a women's magazine editor rejects such a condition, and the publicist won't budge, negotiation breaks down. When this happens, magazines can either go back to the drawing board and find another celeb, or simply employ the "write around." A write-around is where a celeb story is written without an interview or photo shoot. Previously published quotes and secondary sources are used to compile the article, and photos are supplied by paparazzi or a photo agency. This practice, widely used at tabloid publications, is not often approved in the glossies since it damages a magazine editor's relationship with the celebrity publicists, making it unlikely the publicist will accommodate that magazine in the future, essentially blackballing the publication.

One celebrity interviewer shared that in an *Esquire* feature on Kevin Spacey at least ten years back, the writer was very "wink, wink, nudge, nudge" about Spacey's sexual orientation, trying to go for the big buzz. And while the interviewer never came out point-blank and said, "Here's a fact, readers: Kevin Spacey is gay," he did everything but.[10] It was widely talked about within writer and publicist circles at the time. And no doubt Spacey and his own publicist were likely furious. The writer was probably blackballed among celeb publicists for burning a bridge and revealing such a bombshell. And sadly, Spacey didn't do another interview for several years.

But in the women's glossies, celebrities pretty much understand they'll only have to proffer up enough personal information and dish only about "safe" topics (mostly their latest projects). This isn't the kind of *Esquire* or *Playboy* interview where the celebrity opens their closet of skeletons and bleeds out their most personal private struggles on the page, discussing alcoholism battles or eating disorders, sexual abuse or scandal. No, that's not for women's magazines, which generally dish up Pollyanna pieces month after month.

Why don't our glossy magazines run more revealing, intimate, edgy, even intense interviews? If *Esquire* can open these celebs up, why don't our lady-mags do the same? Well, that's a complex issue that has a lot to do with the fluffier style of our glossies, plus the trade-off to promote whatever the celebrity is hawking, whether that's a new TV show, album, movie, clothing line, perfume, philanthropic cause, or anything else. The magazine is often simply the vehicle to promote the celebrity's fill-in-the-blank project, rather than provide any real journalistic look into the makings or mind of the star.

It's a paint-by-numbers formula that is so standard in women's glossies, the interviews seem oddly familiar each month. The hoped-for takeaway? That we trusting readers will then run out to see their movie, read their new memoir, download their music, tune into their hit television show. Of course, after we've bought the issue of the magazine they appeared in. It's a win-win, for all involved.

"I suspect one of the reasons I have never gone after women's magazines, per se, and maybe they haven't gone after me," says celebrity writer Betsy Model, is that A, they edit the crap out of stuff, and B, women's magazines are far more worried about the gloss factor, trying to pigeonhole or get their angle in, whether it's about weight, beauty routine, or plastic surgery. There is a formulaic feeling to the pieces, whether it's Valerie Bertinelli, Jennifer Aniston, or Angelica Houston; it's very surface."

The formula is pretty straightforward, and always includes details about her diet and exercise routine. If the celeb interview has a health or fitness slant, or appears in a health or fitness mag, we learn what the star does or doesn't do to keep her fabulous figure intact. If she's rail thin, she's generally referred to as fit, and if she happens to be buxom and tushy, they call her curvy. On the off-chance her body isn't up for discussion (hello Melissa McCarthy or Oprah in a heavier stage), her body is simply ignored.

Next up, we usually learn how humble and unassuming the actress or singer is. They'll be a great quote or two about how she's just a regular down-to-earth person like we are. Occasionally, to show how edgy or unpretentious the celeb is, the interview will include the requisite F-bombs. You'll find celebs swearing a blue streak more often in *Allure, Cosmo,* or *Vogue* than in *Ladies' Home Journal,* to be sure.

Then there's the personal relationship: the marriage, the boyfriend, or—unlike with most male actors—the trendy admission that she is bisexual. That's a provocative reveal, one for which you can almost imagine the editor pulling a fist pump in her office. In the December 2011 issue of *Women's Health,* for instance, the interview with Amber Heard makes a big deal of the actresses' sexuality, quoting her looking for relationships with the right person, regardless of their gender, and claiming she doesn't really have a sexual orientation. If Heard herself isn't hot enough a celebrity to inspire a big uptake in newsstand sales for that issue, her sexuality disclosure certainly is.

But regardless of a celebrity's sexual orientation, her relationship status is still part of the formula: who's her latest beau? Just how bad was the split with her ex? And how blissful is life with her current romantic interest? The piece will often touch on their cohabiting status or their new home, and how they schedule downtime together.

We learn about any beauty routines the celeb touts, such as her favorite spa for a facial or her most-loved lip balm. We learn what her guilty pleasure is, like reading trashy romance novels or watching raunchy horror flicks. The more banal personality tidbits, the better.

If the celeb's project is working with a hot leading man, an up-and-coming B-list celebrity, or a seasoned older actress, the piece usually delves into how erotic the love scenes were with the actor, how down-to-earth and likeable the young actress like Miley Cyrus or Dakota Fanning is, or how incredibly warm and gracious the seasoned veteran like Meryl or Helen were on set.

By the time we're done reading the interview, we've learned whether the celeb has a reputation for being a diva or a nice girl, and where that rep comes from. We're also likely to hear her take on cosmetic surgery. This falls into the same must-ask question milieu as what she eats and how she stays trim. Whatever her answer, there's often the gracious caveat that it should always be "whatever makes *you* happy." If she's single, she's asked if she's itching to be married and if she is childless, she is asked the perennial question about whether she wants to be a mommy someday. We usually meet her dogs, or at the very least, hear about how many she has acquired to date, though for some reason, not many celebs mention cat ownership. Apparently, dogs are cooler when it comes to the celebrity interview. Either that or many celebs keep cat ownership on the QT.

The piece will then generally wrap on an upnote, with the celebrity offering up some bit of her personal wisdom on life or happiness, family, success, or relationships, leaving us feeling inspired.

"I think there is a formula, and I think that's a shame. Women are smarter readers than some women's magazines give them credit for," says Model.

Do you feel like you've read every celebrity interview ever written in a woman's magazine? That's because you probably have.

THE INTERVIEW PORTION OF THE PROGRAM

While most women's magazines have a few defining characteristics that distinguish them from each other (think *Cosmo* and sex versus *MORE* and aging), they all tend to follow the standard celebrity interview formula laid out above. Let's take a look.

In the December 2011 issue of *Elle,* a magazine that often includes lofty writing and stellar articles among the typical beauty must-haves, the writer interviews Jessica Biel in a piece dubbed "The Real Biel." The six-page spread showcases Biel as the star of an upcoming new movie, *New Year's Eve,* out that month. The article takes the reader through the typical paint-by-numbers formula.

Biel has had a lot of rejection. When asked about the part that got away, she mentions many, including the movie *The Notebook* and the role of Catwoman in the next *Batman* sequel, a part she particularly wanted. She also says that for any female part, there are thirty talented actresses vying for the role. The interviewer touches on her on-again, off-again relationship with Justin Timberlake, in which she claims she really can't elaborate, since some things need to be kept private (as of this writing, they are engaged). She's then asked if she liked wearing the pregnancy belly pad in the movie and if she'd like to be pregnant some day. Sure, she says. But there is no pressure. So far, so good, as far as meeting the formula goes.

Then we switch over to how she's dated a lot of actors. Is that a conscious choice? And—here it comes—we slip into her health, weight, and stamina by mentioning her climb of Mt. Kilimanjaro, a fitness and spiritual adventure Biel took that year. And of course, we conclude with a bit of woo-woo wisdom, where Biel tells readers she lost her cell phone on the mountain, saying the mountain "ate it" because she is supposed to be disconnected while climbing. Touchdown! The interview is a color-within-the-lines success.

In the same vein, *Vogue,* another mag with ingenious writers and lengthier, less fluffy content, captures Charlize Theron at a Japanese restaurant in its December 2011 issue. Regardless of the higher-quality wordsmithing than what's found in other lady-mags, it's nonetheless the same formula; just another restaurant, different celebrity.

Here, the writer begins with the warnings about Theron being a prankster who doesn't take herself too seriously, who can outdrink you, and has an affinity for, wait for it, F-bombs. She is so unpretentious and easygoing it's hard to remember she is a star. Sound familiar? Her latest project, *Young Adults*, is about to hit theaters, hence the reason she is this month's cover girl. Plus, she rocks whatever she wears, and her sultry elegance is a natural fit for *Vogue*. Total coup for all concerned, including her fans. But still, the interview follows a predictable pattern.

After gushing about her career to date and long-lost high school loves, the piece segues into the demise of her ten-year relationship.

Since *Vogue's* more in-depth interviews tend to cover more ground, the writer meets with Theron over several days, at an ice cream parlor, on a hike with her two dogs, and then with a visit to her home, a Spanish colonial hidden behind an unpretentious gate. During the hike, we hear about her current dog addiction and former smoking addiction. She has quit smoking, but won't disclose the method used since it could jinx the process. In an upcoming project (*Snow White and the Huntsman*), she works with Kristen Stewart of *Twilight* fame and naturally waxes on about her younger, more naive costar.

We briefly hit on her warm relationship with her mom and dish up the decades-old scandal in which her mother killed her alcoholic father in self-defense. If you're a celeb, you unfortunately can never get away from a scandal. Call it the Hugh Grant effect.

Shirley MacLaine provides a few comments (the older generation continually must comment on the up-and-comers) just like Theron remarked on Stewart. We learn Theron can cook and throw great dinner parties. In this homey setting, it is a must-ask about whether she wants children.

Of course she does, but no rush.

While the writing is a bit edgier and wider-ranging than some of our other glossies, it nonetheless breaks little from the formula, including the great publicity it generates for her upcoming project.

Likewise, in the December 2011 issue of *Allure,* we meet Lea Michele, the girl behind the honeyed voice of the hit show *Glee.* Naturally, we begin at a cozy table for two in a New York City restaurant. After comparing Michele to Streisand in both talent and vulnerability, we learn Michele has been reported to be a diva from several sources, but only in the true Italian sense of the word—an extraordinary vocal talent.

Aside from playing Rachel Berry in the third season of *Glee,* Michele is starring in the aforementioned movie *New Year's Eve* with Jessica Biel (out at the time of this writing), making this celeb interview and cover girl a particularly hot B-lister. We also learn Michele is Ashton Kutcher's love interest in the film. Kutcher, who is at the height of his popularity for having both the balls to try to breathe life into the fledging hit *Two and a Half Men* after Charlie Sheen's jump-the-shark year, and the Twitter-heavy demise of his relationship with Demi Moore, is the sixth degree of separation the *Glee* star needs to be transformed into a bankable B-lister for the magazine cover.

Michele is the perfect celeb for the plastic surgery debate, because when she was fifteen, a talent manager told her to get a nose job. But her mother put the kibosh on that idea by pointing out that Streisand never got a nose job, and look at her. The interview then touches on reports that Michele got scarily thin the year before and was rumored to have an eating disorder, and then it seamlessly ends with news about Michele's break-up from her two-year relationship with her Broadway actor boyfriend, with whom she's pleased to say she is still friends. She also waxes poetic about Gwyneth Paltrow, a recurring guest star on *Glee*.

Since *Allure* is a beauty mag, the accompanying sidebar includes Michele's beauty secrets with the star's faves and raves about skin, makeup, hair, body, and fragrance products. The interview wraps with the usual look at the actresses' future, mentioning Michele's seven-year contract on *Glee*. She then orders a second dirty martini. Fade to black.

GLOSSY FACT

A 2009 study by MEDIAEDGE:CIA found that 30 percent of respondents aged 18 to 34 would try a product promoted by an admired celebrity compared to 14 percent of those in the 35–54 age group. Additionally, 5 percent of respondents believe celebrity endorsements improve a brand's awareness, help define its personality, and generate interest.[11]

See the formula? There's nothing journalistically wrong with these interviews, except that it's fluff incarnate. The writer hits the assignment nail on the proverbial head by offering everything the magazine editor requested. But wouldn't someone like to know what *Michele* thinks about her nose and how she felt when a talent manager recommended a nose job? Might readers wonder why Theron isn't ever asked her opinion on how to empower women involved in domestic violence, given what she witnessed with her mom? And Biel, mentioning more collective rejection than any actor usually admits to, is not once asked how she truly handles that, if it ever gets her down, or if she thought it might be easier to nab roles at this stage of her career? Nope. Hell, wouldn't we love to hear about something *outside the formula,* like her deeper spiritual beliefs, world affairs, art, or politics? Something of substance . . . anything at all? Instead, the women's magazines choose what to dish up and what to keep mum, as though anything heavy, deep, or analytical would be too cumbersome or lofty for their readership. What do they take us for? Anyone find it a little insulting that when profiling a celebrity, magazines believe we'd rather hear about her favorite lip gloss than something touching or meaningful? Model, who writes mainly for men's and general interest magazines, says she never has an agenda when she does a celebrity interview, nor does she even formulate questions in advance. Her editors and producers expect she'll get great tidbits and unparalleled disclosure not seen before, and she does, without a glossy formula to go by. "Chances are, I didn't get asked to do the interview to ask about the boyfriend or the breakup or their bedtime routine for cleansing their face." Do other magazines do it differently?

DO DICK SLICKS DO IT BETTER?

That brings us to men's magazines, which take a different approach to the celebrity profile. While lad mags are notoriously misogynistic, filled with bawdy humor and sexualizing far too many half-clad women in their pages to be held up as an example of a great magazine, the celebrity interview is, in contrast, handled with a varied approach of depth, wit, respect, and intelligence that's largely missing from most chick slicks. *GQ* and *Esquire*, perhaps even *Playboy,* deliver profiles of a higher caliber, working from the assumption that their readers are educated, savvy, and worldly in a way that women's journals simply don't.

Readers Respond

"I love *Esquire*. The writing is on par with literary mags like *Vanity Fair* or *The Atlantic,* and I find the reporting to be top-notch as well. There are no women's mags that can compare. *Esquire* seems to be designed for a thinking man, while the women's magazines don't seem to have a clue that women have brains."

—Hilda, writer

Some years back, probably as reading articles online became a more popular activity, women's magazines decided that women had short attention spans, and there was a movement to shorten content. Feature articles that ran five to six pages were slashed in half, and featurettes (two- to three-page stories) were slashed with it, making virtually no article longer than the requisite one or two pages in most women's magazines. Dick slicks did not follow this formula. They're still running the eight-page personality profile. But this sad state of affairs continues today. The shallow reasoning behind these changes is that women are time crunched, women read in sound bites, women only glance through an article, so it better be shorter or they won't even consider using their limited time and multitasking brainpower to endure such a reading task. How insulting! Worse, when women's magazines do tackle an important or serious interview, the writing is often humorless or sanctimonious.

"I have women friends who routinely read *Esquire* and *Details*; frankly the writing is a little smarter, hipper, or cheekier. Not that *Cosmo* wouldn't consider themselves cheeky because they talk about orgasms, but I am far more intrigued as a general rule by profiles done in business or men's magazines, or of course, *Vanity Fair*, than I am by what's in the women's magazines. Women's magazine interviews are often dumbed down and boring," says Model.

In the December 2011 issue of *GQ,* for instance, we find a heart-breaking vignette about Amy Winehouse, in which the stoned singer riffs to a reporter in one of her last interviews about how she is written off by friends and family, even the public, because she is a drug addict. At the same time, she laments a quasi-hope that she can emerge from her drug-induced psychosis in time to create more great music. Its poignancy is nothing we could find in a chick slick. The cover girl, Mila Kunis, warrants a one-page quirky spread in the issue, in which the writer spends the whole page telling us how he had a cold and Kunis makes it her duty to make him better (no sick joke intended). They head to a Japanese restaurant for miso soup, a drug store for some kick-ass cough syrup she swears by, and then to her apartment to brew up a home-made concoction consisting of a pricey cab, half a bottle of vodka, a few gel caps of fish oil, and green tea powder for good measure. Again, this type of eccentric interview isn't what we find in the women's magazines. In our glossy neighborhood, Kunis would be asked about her love life, her desire to be a mom, and her favorite beauty must-haves. Next up is the "25 Least Influential People Alive," a hysterical glance into a list of this year's wannabe's, has-beens, derelicts, and been-there's that leaves the reader busting a gut in laughter while feeling mildly uncomfortable for a couple of the people named, even if they do include Arnold Schwarzenegger and Hank Williams Jr., and it's clearly tongue-in-cheek.

An excellent interview with Jay-Z, in which he openly speaks about the loss of his father at age eleven and the anger and loneliness he suffered as a result of his dad's disappearance, almost candidly wishing his father had died before he was born so he could have been spared the deprivation of the loss, is heart wrenching. Although part of the interview takes place at a restaurant, it is merely a meeting ground, and Jay-Z isn't once asked about his eating habits. Missing also is what he ordered off the menu. Likewise, there is no love-life talk or favorite product mentions, though the man is married to one of the most famous women in the music industry and surely uses soap and sunscreen.

While *GQ* is far from perfect and more like a locker room full of adolescent boys when it comes to how they approach women in general, the cover shot of Kunis, in particular, looks like her boobs might have gotten a job. Her normal A-cups appear to be airbrushed into formidable Cs. And while this dick slick deserves a tsk-tsk for her digitized breast enhancement, *GQ* nonetheless deserves kudos for fleshing out her interview with more substance, freshness, and quirky intimacy.

* * *

If only women's magazines would tackle celeb interviews with more zest and grit, readers might not only get more substance but appreciate the celebrity more, as well as the magazine that carries it. Women's magazines insist on keeping these pieces based in fluff, rooted in softball questions, and formulaically set up and laid out in the exact same manner month after month. Further, the pieces are degraded with sexist questions such as the "Do you want to be married," "Be a mother," "Eat only vegetables"—crap that cements the profiles in mediocrity bordering on mindlessness.

But can't women's magazines find a way to showcase beautiful fashions, the latest accessories, and offer up beautifully written, humorous takes, or in-depth analyses on celebs that actually mean something? Women crave stories that touch their hearts or invade their souls rather than pieces that take each celeb at such shallow face value. Women are begging for their magazines to dig a little deeper beneath the surface and come up with something new or original when it comes to a celebrity. These types of changes can only make women's magazines shine, endearing reader loyalty. Yet they choose to continue taking the low road. Would one of our chick slicks even consider basing a profile on hanging out with Kunis and making a cold remedy? How about asking the rich and famous, the talented and artistic, the creative and the inventive, something other than their favorite moisturizer, lady mags? Women the world over will thank you!

Notes

CHAPTER 1: A CHICK-SLICK HISTORY

1. Mary Ellen Zuckerman, *A History of Popular Women's Magazines in the United States* (Praeger, July 1998).

2. Tracy Seneca, "The History of Women's Magazines: Magazines as Virtual Communities," graduate thesis, New York Univeristy, Fall 1993, http://besser.tsoa.nyu.edu/impact/f93/students/tracy/tracy_hist.html.

3. Kristin H. Gerhard, "International Women's Periodicals: Eighteenth Century to the Great Depression," International Women's Periodicals, Cornell University library archive online, http://iwp.library.cornell.edu/i/iwp/women_intro.html.

4. Seneca, "The History of Women's Magazines."

5. Zuckerman, *A History of Popular Women's Magazines,* 3.

6. "Magazines and Publications II," funtrivia.com, http://www.funtrivia.com/en/subtopics/Magazines-and-Publications-II-81154.html.

7. Zuckerman, *A History of Popular Women's Magazines,* 46.

8. Zuckerman, *A History of Popular Women's Magazines,* 48.

9. Zuckerman, *A History of Popular Women's Magazines,* 51.

10. Zuckerman, *A History of Popular Women's Magazines,* 88.

11. Zuckerman, *A History of Popular Women's Magazines,* 117.

12. Zuckerman, *A History of Popular Women's Magazines,* 205.

13. Zuckerman, *A History of Popular Women's Magazines,* 108.

14. Zuckerman, *A History of Popular Women's Magazines,* 138.

15. Ibid.

16. Zuckerman, *A History of Popular Women's Magazines,* 146.

17. Zuckerman, *A History of Popular Women's Magazines,* 55.

18. Zuckerman, *A History of Popular Women's Magazines,* 93 – 95.

19. Ibid.

20. Ibid.

21. Zuckerman, *A History of Popular Women's Magazines,* 208-209.

22. Zuckerman, *A History of Popular Women's Magazines,* 219.

23. Zuckerman, *A History of Popular Women's Magazines,* 220.

24. Ibid.

25. Michelle Tauber, "The War of the Rosies," *People* magazine online, October 2, 2002, http://www.people.com/people/archive/article/0,,20138165,00.html.

26. Ibid.

27. Anne Moore, "Transformation 2010: A Message from Magazine Leaders," opening remarks, Transformation 2010, American Association of Advertising Agencies, February 28, 2010, http://www.aaaa.org/events/transcripts/Pages/030110_MagLeadersAM.aspx.

CHAPTER 2: THE PINK GHETTO

1. Carol Kleiman, "Pink Collar Workers Fight to Leave 'Ghetto,'" *The Seattle Times* online archive, January 8, 2006, http://seattletimes.nwsource.com/html/businesstechnology/2002727003_kleiman08.html?syndication=rss.

2. "The Devil Wears Prada?" All About Anna Wintour, blogspot, http://12-anna-wintour.blogspot.com/p/devil-wears-prada.html (accessed February 2012).

3. Melissa Kent, "In a High-Gloss, High-Heeled Hell, Maghag's Blog is Baring Fashion's Nasty Secrets," *The Age Newspaper* online, May 8, 2008,

http://www.theage.com.au/news/national/baring-fashions-nasty-se-crets/2008/05/17/1210765260552.html?page=fullpage.

4. Linda Wells, "Letter from the Editor," *Allure* magazine, May 2011.

5. Ibid.

6. Irin Carmen, "Sex Sells: The Cosmo-fication of Women's Health," Jezebel, December 11, 2009, http://jezebel.com/5424434/sex-sells-the-cosmo+fication-of-womens-health.

7. Samir Husni, "Simplify and 9 other tips I learned from the new Woman's Day," Mr. Magazine blog, June 4, 2007, http://mrmagazine.word-press.com/2007/06/page/2/.

8. Ibid.

9. Lucia Moses, "As Seventeen Goes Upscale, Can it Keep its Readers?" *Adweek* online, March 15, 2011, http://www.adweek.com/news/televi-sion/seventeen-goes-upscale-can-it-keep-its-readers-125996.

10. Nicole Breane, "40 Years Of Feminist Journalism Courtesy of *Ms.* Magazine," Zelda Lilly blog, January 30, 2012, http://zeldalily.com/index.php/2012/01/40-years-of-feminist-journalism-courtesy-of-ms-magazine/.

11. Alicia Lukachko and Elizabeth M. Whelan, "Popular Women's Maga-zines are Still Downplaying the Risks of Smoking," American Council on Science and Health, March 1, 1999, http://www.acsh.org/publications/pubID.415/pub_detail.asp.

12. Nat Ives, "Lawmaker Who Attacked Mags Over Cig Ads Isn't Happy With Response," *Ad Age* online, August 16, 2007, http://adage.com/ar-ticle/media/lawmaker-attacked-mags-cig-ads-happy-response/119899/.

13. Alison Stein Wellner, "Why Magazines Suck," Media column, Huff-ington Post, January 16, 2009, http://www.huffingtonpost.com/alison-stein-wellner/why-magazines-suck_b_158565.htm.

14. "Scent Research," Whiff Solutions, AskTheWhiffGuys.com, 2008, http://www.whiffsolutions.com/research.html.

15. PRNewswire, "Size Does Matter Especially When Combined with In-novation and Creative Execution," The Free Library online, February 26,

2007, http://www.thefreelibrary.com/New+GfK+Starch(R)+Report+Reveals+the+Power+of+%27Spectacular%27+Ads.-a0159792471.

16. "Impulse Selling through Package Smelling," blog post by Liz, askthewhiffguys.com, May 27, 2008, http://askthewhiffguys.com/research/case-studies/impulse-selling-through-package-smelling-2/.

17. Bruce Horowitz, "Dollars and Scents : Some Magazines Are Rethinking Those Perfume Ads," Los Angeles Times online, Marketing section, November 17, 1992, http://articles.latimes.com/1992-11-17/business/fi-603_1_perfume-ads.

18. P Kumar, et al, "Inhalation Challenge Effects of Perfume Scent Strips in Patients with Asthma," *Annals of Allergy, Asthma & Immunology* 75, no. 5 (November 1995): 429-33.

19. "Fragrance & Cosmetic Advertisements in Periodicals Publications," Customer Support Ruling, United States Postal Service, September 2005, http://pe.usps.com/text/csr/PS-273.htm.

20. BE Fisher, "Scents and Sensitivity," *Environmental Health Perspectives* 106 (December 1998): 594-599, http://dx.doi.org/10.1289/ehp.98106a594.

21. Ibid.

CHAPTER 3: TRUTH IN ADVERTISING

1. "Beauty and Body Image in the Media," report by the Media Awareness Network, 2006, http://www2.fiu.edu/~surisc/beauty%20and%20body%20image.pdf.

2. Ibid.

3. Ibid.

4. Ibid.

5. Mark Sweney, "L'Oréal's Julia Roberts and Christy Turlington Ad Campaigns Banned," July 26, 2011, http://www.guardian.co.uk/media/2011/jul/27/loreal-julia-roberts-ad-banned.

6. Tara Parker Pope, "The French Rethink Thin," the *New York Times* online, April 15, 2008, http://well.blogs.nytimes.com/2008/04/15/the-french-rethink-thin/.

7. "Kate Moss Mascara Ads Banned after Complaints Her Lashes Were False," The Daily Mail online, October 3, 2007, http://www.dailymail.co.uk/tvshowbiz/article-485333/Kate-Moss-mascara-ads-banned-complaints-lashes-false.html#ixzz1zcJbO3xd.

8. The Subliminal Hypnotist, "Subliminal Advertising: Hoax or Truth," How to Subliminal blog,

http://www.howtosubliminal.com/subliminal-advertising-hoax-truth/.

9. Cheryl Wischhover, "The U.K. ASA Slams a Rachel Weisz for L'Oreal Ad for 'Unrealistic Retouching,'" February 21, 2012, adhttp://fashionista.com/2012/02/the-uks-asa-slams-a-rachel-weisz-for-loreal-ad-for-unrealistic-retouching/.

10. Gloria Steinem, "Sex, Lies & Advertising," *Ms. Magazine,* July/August 1990.

11. Ibid.

12. Ibid.

13. Joe Mandese, "Paid Product Placement Surges in Magazines, Newspapers, Other Media," MediaDailyNews online, July 26, 2005, http://www.mediapost.com/publications/article/32440/paid-product-placement-surges-in-magazines-newspa.html.

14. Ibid.

15. Julian Sivulka, *Ad Women: How they Impact What We Need, Want, and Buy* (Prometheus Books, November 2008), 228.

16. Abby Rourke, "The American Housewife: Television and Magazine Images of Middle-Class Women, 1950-1955," graduate thesis, January 30, 2011, Siena College, New York, http://www.siena.edu/uploadedfiles/home/Academics/Schools_and_Departments/School_of_Liberal_Arts/History/Siena_Argus/A.%20Rourke%20Capstone-Final%20Copy.pdf.

17. Sivulka, *Ad Women.*

18. Sivulka, *Ad Women.*

19. Sivulka, *Ad Women.*

20. "Dodge La Femme—Never a Car More Distinctively Feminine," Collector Car Ads blog, February 11, 2009, http://blog.collectorcarads.com/dodge-la-femme/02/2009/.

21. Ibid.

22. Sivulka, *Ad Women,* 342

23. Sivulka, *Ad Women,* 348.

24. Sivulka, *Ad Women,* 358.

CHAPTER 4: FASHION FORWARD

1. Jim Edwards, "Why the FTC Should Sue Harper's Bazaar over Its Fashion Spreads," CBS News online, November 11, 2010, http://www.cbsnews.com/8301-505123_162-42746549/why-the-ftc-should-sue-harpers-bazaar-over-its-fashion-spreads/.

2. Ibid.

3. Jennifer Craik, *The Faces of Fashion: Cultural Studies in Fashion* (Psychology Press, January 1994), 58.

4. Nat Ives, "Vogue's September Issue Leads Fashion Pack with 584 Ad Pages," *Ad Age* Media News online, July 20, 2011, http://adage.com/article/media/vogue-s-september-issue-leads-fashion-pack-584-ad-pages/228826/.

5. Joshua Levine, "Brand Anna," Wall Street Journal online, March 23, 2011, http://online.wsj.com/article/SB10001424052748704893604576200722939264658.html.

6. Lauren Sherman, "Most Powerful Fashion Magazine Editors," *Forbes* Magazine online, September 4, 2008, http://www.forbes.com/2008/09/04/style-editor-magazine-forbeslife-cx_ls_0904editors.html.

7. Ibid.

8. Eric Wilson, "Magazines Begin to Sell the Fashions they Review," *New York Times,* September 25, 2011.

9. Angela Carrol, "Brand Communications in Fashion Categories, Using Celebrity Endorsement," *Journal of Brand Management* 17 (September 12, 2008): 146 – 158.

10. Ariana Finlayson, "Jason Wu for Target Sells At Missoni-Like Speed," *US Weekly,* February 6, 2012, http://www.usmagazine.com/celebrity-style/news/jason-wu-for-target-sells-at-missoni-like-speed-201262.

11. Ibid.

12. Christina Binkley, "How Can Jeans Cost $300?" Wall Street Journal online, July 7, 2011, http://online.wsj.com/article/SB1000142405270230 3365804576429730284498872.html.

13. Ksenia Kahnovich, "Fashion Talk: Coco Rocha Supports the Model Alliance Created by a Model Sara Ziff," Top Fashion Style blog, February 6, 2012, http://topfashionstyle.com/fashion-news/fashion-talk-coco-ro-cha-supports-the-model-alliance-created-by-a-model-sara-ziff.

14. Sarah Ziff, *Picture Me: A Model's Diary,* documentary film (Strand Releasing, January 11, 2011).

15. Ibid.

16. Amy Odell, "Anna Wintour, Michael Kors, and Natalia Vodianova Discussed Eating Disorders in Boston," *New York Magazine* online, March 23, 2010, http://nymag.com/daily/fashion/2010/03/anna_wintour_mi-chael_kors_and.html.

17. Sarah Weir, "Cindy Crawford Pulls Plug on 10-Year-Old Daughter's Modeling Career," Yahoo! Shine fashion news, February 16, 2012, http://shine.yahoo.com/fashion/cindy-crawford-pulls-plug-ten-old-daugh-ter-8217-183000108.html.

18. Olivia Bergen, "Dakota Fanning's Oh, Lola! advert for Marc Jacobs is banned," *The Telegraph UK* online, http://fashion.telegraph.co.uk/article/TMG8876913/Dakota-Fannings-Oh-Lola-advert-for-Marc-Jacobs-is-banned.html.

19. Nina Jones, "Marc Jacobs' Oh, Lola Ad Banned in U.K.," *Women's Wear Daily* online, November 9, 2011, http://www.wwd.com/beauty-indus-try-news/fragrance/marc-jacobs-oh-lola-ad-banned-5358741.

20. Sheila Marikar, "Kate Upton: Sports Illustrated Darling, but Not Fit for Victoria's Secret," ABCNews.com, February 15, 2012, http://abcnews.go.com/blogs/entertainment/2012/02/kate-upton-sports-illustrated-darling-but-not-fit-for-victorias-secret/.

21. Emily Blaha, "The Portrayal of Women in Magazine Advertisements Across Four Different Women's Magazines," *Journal for the Human Sciences* Volume 5 (2006). http://www.kon.org/urc/v5/blaha.html.

22. "Statistics: Easting Disorders and their Precursors," Fact Sheet, National Eating Disorders Association, 2005, http://www.sc.edu/healthycarolina/pdf/facstaffstu/eatingdisorders/EatingDisorderStatistics.pdf.

23. Alan, Wirzbicki, "Fashion Designers Need to Stop Blaming Models for the Industry's Anorexia Problem," The Angle blog, *Boston Globe* online, February 9, 2012, http://www.boston.com/bostonglobe/editorial_opinion/blogs/the_angle/2012/02/fashion_designe.html.

24. A. Preti, et al, "Eating disorders among professional fashion models," *Journal of Psychiatry Research* 159, no. 1-2 (May 30, 2008): 86–94.

25. Wirzbicki, "Fashion Designers Need to Stop Blaming Models," *Boston Globe.*

26. Ian Sparks and Ben Tod, "'She is a little too fat': Karl Lagerfeld slates Adele's size before backtracking on his comments about her image," The Daily Mail online, February 8, 2012, http://www.dailymail.co.uk/tvshowbiz/article-2097488/Karl-Lagerfeld-slates-Adeles-image-backtracking-comments.html.

27. Jenna Sauers, "Karl Lagerfeld Is Very Sorry He Called Adele Fat," Jezebel, February 8, 2012, http://jezebel.com/5883434/karl-lagerfeld-is-very-sorry-he-called-adele-fat.

CHAPTER 5: IT AIN'T ABOUT INNER BEAUTY

1. Anna Holmes, "Memo To Women's Magazine Editors: White Women Hate Themselves After Reading Your Magazines," Jezebel, March 30,

2007, http://jezebel.com/248484/memo-to-womens-magazine-editors-white-women-hate-themselves-after-reading-your-magazines.

2. Rebecca Reisner, "The Diet Industry: A Big Fat Lie," *Businessweek* online, The Debate Room blog, January 10, 2008, http://www.businessweek.com/debateroom/archives/2008/01/the_diet_indust.html.

3. "Healthy Weight: It's Not a Diet, It's a Lifestyle," Fact Sheet, Center for Disease Control and Prevention online, http://www.cdc.gov/healthy-weight/calories/index.html.

4. Roger Gould, MD, "Why Diets Fail," Yahoo! Voices, Dieting and Weight Loss blog, December 18, 2007, http://voices.yahoo.com/why-diets-fail-725647.html.

5. Ibid.

6. Shaun Dreisbach, "Shocking Body-Image News: 97% of Women Will Be Cruel to Their Bodies Today," *Glamour* online, February 18, 2011, http://www.glamour.com/health-fitness/2011/02/shocking-body-image-news-97-percent-of-women-will-be-cruel-to-their-bodies-today#ixzz1znerEjO3 2.

7. "Three Out Of Four American Women Have Disordered Eating, Survey Suggests," ScienceDaily.com, April 8, 2008, http://www.sciencedaily.com/releases/2008/04/080422202514.htm.

8. Susan Lundman, "What Happens to a Woman's Body at 40?" LiveStrong.com, May 26, 2011, http://www.livestrong.com/article/363851-what-happens-to-a-womens-body-at-40/#ixzz1p8DQ6qqc.

9. Aisha Tyler, "I Don't Want to Be Perfect," *Glamour,* September 2005.

10. Lucy Danziger, "Do We Retouch? Yes!" *Self* online, Lucy's Blog, August 10, 2009, http://www.self.com/magazine/blogs/lucysblog/2009/08/pictures-that-please-us.html.

11. "Glamour Responds to 'Skinny Betty' Charges!" Aaaay! Starlets blog, September 7, 2007, http://ayyyy.com/glamour-responds-to-skinny-betty-charges/.

12. "This Week in Kerfuffle: The Faith Hill / Redbook Controversy," That Was Probably Awkward blog, July 24, 2007, http://probablyawkward.typepad.com/that_was_probably_awkward/2007/07/this-week-in-ke.html.

13. Anna Holmes, "Faith Hill's 'Redbook' Photoshop Chop: Why We're Pissed," Jezebel, July 17, 2007, http://jezebel.com/279203/faith-hills-red-book-photoshop-chop-why-were-pissed.

14. Dreisbach, "Shocking Body Image News," *Glamour.*

15. "As Mainstream Media Decline, Niche and Foreign Outlets Grow," The Washington Press Corp: A Special Report, The Pew Center for Excellence in Journalism, July 16, 2009, http://www.journalism.org/analysis_report/new_washington_press_corps.

16. Rosie Molinary, author of *Beautiful You: A Daily Guide to Radical Self-Acceptance* (Seal Press, October 2010).

17. Jennifer Romolini, "Yay! French *Elle*'s Amazing No-Makeup Issue (and why American mags need to step it up)," Yahoo! Shine, April 14, 2009, http://shine.yahoo.com/fashion/yay-french-elles-amazing-no-makeup-issue-and-why-american-mags-need-to-step-it-up-446538.html.

18. Melinda Brodbeck and Erin Evans, "Dove Campaign for Real Beauty Case Study," Public Relations Problems and Cases blog, Pennsylvania State University, March 5, 2007, http://psucomm473.blogspot.com/2007/03/dove-campaign-for-real-beauty-case.html.

19. Jessica Bennett, "Weighty Matters," The Daily Beast, February 7, 2007, http://www.thedailybeast.com/newsweek/2007/02/07/weighty-matters.html.

20. Jessica Bennett, "Picture Perfect," The Daily Beast, May 1, 2008, http://www.thedailybeast.com/newsweek/2008/05/01/picture-perfect.html.

21. Emma Brownell, "Dove's Evolution Video Drives Debate," iMedia-Connection.com, October 24, 2006, http://www.imediaconnection.com/content/11841.asp.

22. Lauren Collins, "Pixel Perfect: Pascal Danzig's Virtual Reality," *The New Yorker,* May 12, 2008.

23. "First Thing Women Notice About Other Women is How FAT They Are," *Daily Mail UK* online, May 27, 2011, http://www.dailymail.co.uk/femail/article-1391477/Women-pass-judgement-20-seconds-meeting-them.html.

24. Collins, "Pixel Perfect," *The New Yorker.*

25. Ibid.

26. Eric Kee and Hany Farid, "A Perceptual Metric for Photo Retouching," *Proceedings of the National Academy of Sciences,* November 28, 2011, http://www.pnas.org/content/early/2011/11/21/1110747108.abstract.

27. Camilla Long, "Pascal Dangin: The Master Manipulator," The Fashion Spot blog, May 18, 2008, http://forums.thefashionspot.com/f71/pascal-dangin-photo-retoucher-80052.html.

CHAPTER 6: TO AGE OR NOT TO AGE

1. Theresa Ruth Howard, "Beauty and Body Image in the Media," My Body My Image blog, February 13, 2012, http://www.mybodymyimage.com/beauty-and-body-image-in-the-media.

2. Stephanie Pappas, "Magazines' Youthful Ideal Threatens Real Women's Sexuality," LiveScience, June 12, 2011, http://www.livescience.com/14562-fashion-magazines-vogue-older-women-sexuality.html.

3. Ibid.

4. Ibid.

5. "U.S. Consumers Quest to Remain Forever Young Driving Growth in $12.4 Billion Cosmeceuticals Market, According to New Report," *Cosmetic Surgery News*, January 18, 2008, http://www.cosmeticsurgery-news.com/article2385.html.

6. Mike Adams, "Quest for Eternal Youth Credited With Rising Cosmetic Sales," NaturalNews.com, January 25, 2005, http://www.naturalnews.com/003802.html#ixzz1zr38zJoE.

7. "Surveys Find Many Young Women Begin Planning Plastic Surgeries in Teens," The American Society for Aesthetic Plastic Surgery, September 19, 2011, http://www.surgery.org/consumers/plastic-surgery-news-briefs/surveys-find-young-women-planning-plastic-surgeries-teens-1035572.

8. Ibid.

9. Wendy Felton, "*InStyle*'s Insane Ideas About Women's Bodies," Glossed Over blog post, September 9, 2008, http://www.glossedover.com/glossed_over/2008/09/instyles-insane.html.

10. Stephanie Clifford, "The Readers Are Over 40 (Don't Tell Advertisers)," *The New York Times,* August 23, 2009, http://www.nytimes.com/2009/08/24/business/media/24more.html?pagewanted=all.

11. Ibid.

12. Ibid.

13. Jessica Bennett, "Generation Diva: How our Obsession with Beauty is Changing Our Kids," The Daily Beast, March 29, 2009, http://www.thedailybeast.com/newsweek/2009/03/29/generation-diva.html

14. Ibid.

15. Ibid.

16. Ibid.

17. Ibid.

18. Ibid.

19. Ibid.

20. Ibid.

21. Ibid.

22. Naomi Wolf, *The Beauty Myth* (Vintage Books, September 1991).

23. Susan Sontag, *The Double Standard of Aging* (Farrar, Straus, & Giroux, Inc; 1979).

24. Tom Chiarella, "What Is a Man?" *Esquire,* April 6, 2009, http://www.esquire.com/features/what-is-a-man-0509#ixzz1pFPitveg.

25. "How a Man Ages, or Should," *Esquire* online, http://www.esquire.com/features/men-aging-well-0610#ixzz1pFV6XuB3 (accessed February 10, 2012).

26. Ibid.

27. Hillari Dowdle, "Natural Born Leaders," *Natural Health Magazine* online, http://www.naturalhealthmag.com/mind-body/natural-born-leaders (accessed February 10, 2012).

28. Bim Adewunmi, "I'm Interested in All the Personal Stuff," *The Guardian UK* newspaper online, June 9, 2011, http://www.guardian.co.uk/life-andstyle/2011/jun/10/jane-pratt-veteran-alternative-glossy.

29. Ibid.

CHAPTER 7: FEMININE FEAR FACTOR

1.Myrna Blyth, *Spin Sisters: How The Women Of The Media Sell Unhappiness—And Liberalism—To The Women Of America* (Macmillan, 2005), 45.

2. Barry Wigmore, "Just Why Are Women Unhappier Than Men?" *The Daily Mail UK* online, September 27, 2007, http://www.dailymail.co.uk/news/article-484134/Just-women-unhappier-men.html.

3. "Health Coverage in Popular Women's Magazines Focuses on an Individual's Initiative, Missouri Journalism Professor Suggests," news release, Missouri School of Journalism, May 28, 2010, http://journalism.missouri.edu/2010/05/health-coverage-in-popular-womens-magazines-focuses-on-an-individuals-initiative-missouri-journalism-professor-suggests/.

4. Ibid.

5. Sherrill Sellman, "Osteoporosis—The Bones of Contention," Health101.org, http://health101.org/art_osteo_bones.htm (accessed November 2011).

6. Lorraine Silver Wallace, PhD, and Joyce E. Ballard, PhD, "Osteoporosis Coverage in Selected Women's Magazines and Newspapers, 1998-2001," *American Journal of Health Behavior* vol. 27 no. 1 (2003): 75-83.

7. "Bone Health and Osteoporosis: A Report of the Surgeon General," U.S. Department of Health and Human Services, October 14, 2004, http://www.surgeongeneral.gov/library/reports/bonehealth/chapter_4.html.

8. "The Nutrition Source: Calcium and Milk: What's Best for Your Bones and Health?" The Harvard School of Public Health fact sheet, http://www.hsph.harvard.edu/nutritionsource/what-should-you-eat/calcium-full-story/ (accessed November 2011).

9. "Serial Murder: Multi-Disciplinary Perspectives for Investigators," Reports and Publications, Federal Bureau of Investigation, http://www.fbi.gov/stats-services/publications/serial-murder (accessed November 2011).

10. Gwen Sharp, PhD, "Missing White Woman Syndrome and Fear of Crime," School of Liberal Arts & Sciences online, Nevada State College, August 1, 2011, http://nsclas.blogspot.com/2011/08/missing-white-woman-syndrome-and-fear.html.

11. Ibid.

12. Barry Glasner, "Narrative Techniques of Fear Mongering," *Social Research* Vol. 72, no. 4 (Winter 2004): 819-826.

13. Ronald Bailey, "Fear Itself," Reason.com, April 12, 2011, http://reason.com/archives/2011/04/12/fear-itself.

CHAPTER 8: TO THE LEFT

1. Philo Wasburn, "Media Coverage of Women in Politics: The Curious Case of Sarah Palin," *Media Culture Society* Vol. 33 no. 7 (October 2011): 1027—1041.

2. Jonathan Van Meter, "In Hillary's Footsteps: Kirstin Gillibrand," *Vogue,* October 2010.

3. Flannel Jesus, "Women and Leftism: An Interesting Google Search," ILovePhilosophy.com, February 24, 2012, http://www.ilovephilosophy.com/viewtopic.php?t=178251.

4. Erin Hatten and Mary Nell Trautner, "Equal Opportunity Objectification? The Sexualization of Men and Women on the Cover of Rolling Stone," *The Journal of Sex and Culture* Vol. 15, no. 3 (2011): 256–278.

5. John Koblin, "Can Todd Make a Mooseburger? Women's Mags Scramble on Palin Coverage," *New York Observer,* September 23, 2008.

6. Jennifer Siebel Newsom, *Miss Representation,* documentary produced by Girls Club Entertainment, October 2011, http://www.missrepresentation.org/the-film/.

7. "The United States Congress: Quick Facts," ThisNation.com, http://thisnation.com/congress-facts.html (accessed February 2012).

8. Jack Demarest and Jeanette Garner, "The Representation of Women's Roles in Women's Magazines Over the Past 30 Years," *Journal of Psychology: Interdisciplinary and Applied* Vol. 126, no. 4 (Jul 1992): 357–368.

9. Ibid.

10. Jenn Goddu, "'Powerless, Public-Spirited Women,' 'Angry Feminists,' and 'The Muffin Lobby': Newspaper and Magazine Coverage of the Canadian Advisory Council on the Status of Women, the National Action Committee on the Status of Women, and REAL Women of Canada," *Canadian Journal of Communication* Vol. 24, no. 1 (1999).

11. *"Details'* Peres On Which Women's Mag He'd Edit: 'I'm Waiting for Cindi to F*ck It All Up At Glamour,'" Mediabistro.com, Fishbowl New York, blog post by "Rebecca," April 30, 2008, http://www.mediabistro.com/fishbowlny/details-peres-on-which-womens-mag-hed-edit-im-waiting-for-cindi-to-fck-it-all-up-at-glamour_b8601.

12. Elaine Ray, "Stanford Symposium, Exhibits, Talk by Gloria Steinem Commemorate *Ms.* Magazine's 40 Years," *The Stanford Report,* Stanford Univeristy, January 9, 2012, http://news.stanford.edu/news/2012/january/stanford-ms-magazine-010912.html.

13. Sheila Weller, "Time to Have a Little Talk about Those Women's Magazines," Huffington Post, December 30, 2008, http://www.huffingtonpost.com/sheila-weller/time-to-have-a-little-tal_b_154223.html.

14. Arwa Aburawa, "Revisiting Marie Claire's Coverage of Muslim Women," Patheos.com, MuslimahMediaWatch blog, September 20, 2010, http://www.patheos.com/blogs/mmw/2010/09/finding-a-balance-between-critique-and-praise-revisiting-marie-claires-coverage-of-muslim-women/.

15. Ibid.

16. "American Mothers are Primary Influence on Women's Political Behavior and Attitudes,Oxygen/Markle Pulse Finds," news release, The Markle Foundation, June 30, 2000, http://www.markle.org/news-events/media-

releases/american-mothers-are-primary-influence-womens-political-behavior-and-atti.

17. Kalia Doner, "Surely Life's Not as Bad as the Magazine's Say?" *Chicago Tribune,* August 22, 1993, http://articles.chicagotribune.com/1993-08-22/features/9308220009_1_working-mother-working-woman-feminist-ideas.

18. "Women's Magazines:A Liberal Pipeline to Soccer Moms," special report, Media Research Center, November 21, 1996, http://archive.mrc.org/specialreports/1996/sr19961121.asp.

19. Blythe, *Spin Sisters,* 261-2.

20. "Women's Magazines: A Liberal Pipeline," Media Research Center (see no. 18).

21. "Record High 67 Percent See Political Bias in News Media," blog post, Media Research Center, February 15, 2012, http://www.mrc.org/media-bias-101/exhibit-2-26-record-high-67-see-political-bias-news-media.

22. Linda Lowen, "Women Talk Politics: Friends Influence Friends," About.com, Women's Issues, http://womensissues.about.com/od/thepoliticalarena/a/discusspolitics_4.htm (accessed February 2012).

CHAPTER 9: THE BIG O

1. Jennifer Thompson, "Sexploitation the Big Seller in the Mass Media," OurWeekly.com, Antelope Valley News, July 14, 2011, http://www.our-weekly.com/los-angeles/sexploitation-big-seller-mass-media.

2. Laura Carpenter, "From Girls into Women: Scripts for Sexuality and Romance in *Seventeen* Magazine, 1974 – 1994," *The Journal of Sex Research* Vol. 35, No. 2 (May 1998): 158–168.

3. Thompson, "Sexploitation the Big Seller," OurWeekly.com.

4. Elaine Welteroff, "Guy Pretty Vs. Girl Pretty," *Glamour* online, http://www.glamour.com/beauty/2012/01/guy-pretty-vs-girl-pretty#slide=9 (accessed February 2012).

5. "Kinsey's Heterosexual-Homosexual Rating Scale," The Kinsey Institute, http://www.iub.edu/~kinsey/research/ak-hhscale.html (accessed March 2012).

6. Gary J. Gates, "How Many People are Lesbian, Gay, Bisexual, and Transgender?" The Williams Institute, UCLA, http://williamsinstitute.law.ucla.edu/wp-content/uploads/Gates-How-Many-People-LGBT-Apr-2011.pdf.

7. Anouk Vleugels, "Research: Bisexuality is Normal for Women," *United Academics Magazine,* October 25, 2011, http://www.united-academics.org/magazine/2272/bisexuality-is-natural-for-women/.

8. Laurie Abraham, "The Pink Ghetto: Why Women's Magazines Get No Respect," Mediabistro panel discussion, October 3, 2002, http://www.mediabistro.com/spotlight/archives/01/10/10/.

9. Christine Ottery, "Video: Quick and Dirty Women's Mags," Women's Mag Science June 18, 2010, http://www.womens-mag-science.com/2010/06/18/video-quick-and-dirty-womens-magazinest/.

10. Ibid.

11. Abraham, "The Pink Ghetto: Why Women's Magazines Get No Respect," (see no. 8 above).

12. Ottery, "Video: Quick and Dirty Women's Mags."

13. Chandra Czape, "The Pink Ghetto? Why Women's Magazines Get No Respect," (see no. 11 above).

CHAPTER 10: CELEBRITY CENTRAL

1. "The Rise and Fall of the Supermodel," Hub Pages, post by Seabastian, March 3, 2010, http://seabastian.hubpages.com/hub/The-Rise-and-Fall-of-the-Supermodel

2. Ibid.

3. "The supermodel is dead, says Claudia Schiffer," *The Daily Mail UK* online, September 3, 2007, http://www.dailymail.co.uk/tvshowbiz/article-479711/The-supermodel-dead-says-Claudia-Schiffer.html.

4. Lucia Moses, "Top-Selling Cover Girls (and Boys) of the Year," *AdWeek* online, April 25, 2011, http://www.adweek.com/news/press/top-selling-cover-girls-and-boys-year-130743.

5. Ibid.

6. John Koblin, "The Cover Story: The Best (and Worst) Sellers of 2011," Women's Wear Daily, December 23, 2011, http://www.wwd.com/media-news/media-features/newsstands-best-and-worst-sellers-of-2011-5441321.

7. Erica Harrison, "Divine Trash: the Psychology of Celebrity Obsession," *Cosmos* Magazine, February 2006, http://www.cosmosmagazine.com/node/414/.

8. Misty Harris, "The Skinny on Celebrities: Study Finds Thin Stars in Magazines May Help Women's Body Image," *Postmedia News,* February 21, 2012, http://www2.canada.com/topics/news/story.html?id=6185933.

9. Elizabeth Hendrickson, "Economic Rationalism: Celebrity Placement in Women's Magazines," *Journal of Magazine and New Media Research* Vol. 11, no. 1 (Fall 2009): 1–15.

10. Betsy Model, personal interview, January 2012.

11. Aaron Baar, "Matching Brands with a Celebrity is a Science," Media-Post Publications Marketing Daily, November 27, 2009, http://www.mediapost.com/publications/marketing-daily/edition/2009/11/27/?print.

Acknowledgments

I'd like to thank the women's magazines for being a source from which I have been partaking, both personally and professionally, for many years, and to all the wonderful women's glossy editors I have had the pleasure of working with over the years—you know who you are. Thank you.

A huge debt of thanks, also, to Jennifer Lawler, without whose vision of something bigger than I could even imagine inspired both the premise and the early discussions of this project. I will always be grateful for your incredible insight and encouragement in making lemonade where I thought there were only lemons.

To Deborah Ritchken, agent extraordinaire, for loving and loathing the women's magazines almost as much as I do, to be able to see this project had merit—and to intuitively take a chance on it with me. For her continued support, ideas, and wisdom, I am very grateful.

To everyone at Seal Press for believing in this project and daring to be bold, while daring me to be bolder. Special thanks to Krissa Lagos and Eva Zimmerman for publicity, and extreme gratitude to Krista Lyons, who has shepherded this book from the beginning. And for giving me Merrik!

To Merrik Bush-Pirkle, my Fairy God Editor, I owe a debt of gratitude for her many hours of hard work, her endless patience, brilliant suggestions, and wisdom in the editing of this project. Merrik waved a magic red pen over many drafts of this book, and without her editing prowess it would not be worth the trees sacrificed.

To the many writers, editors, PR professionals, and readers who were kind and generous enough to offer up comments, interviews, grant permission for the use of their work and their words, and the writing community at large who so supported this project with anticipation and excitement, I thank you. Especially the following: Sandi Sedberry Auten, Jane Boursaw, Lola Augustine Brown, Hilda Brucker, Charmian Christie, Alyson McNutt English, Jennifer Fink, Jaclyn Friedman, Roxanne Hawn, Maralyn Hill, Sandra Hume, Sylvia Jordan, Laura Laing, Ann Leitz, Stacy Lipson, Jen Miller, Betsy Model, Rosie Molinary, Maire Peters, Jennie Phipps, Joan Price, Ligeia Polidora, Andy Purnell, Tracee Sioux, Beverly Solomon, Sharon Anne Waldrop, Nicole Weider, and Allison Stein Wellner.

To the following dear friends and family who always offer their total support and encouragement: Roger and Regina Bryan, Debra Cordner Nelson, and the entire Nelson clan; and of course to my mom of the past eighteen years, Linda Wilson, I thank you for all of your loving support.

Special thanks to Diane Faulkner, who never fails to make me feel like a writing rock star no matter what I write, for her friendship and wise counsel over many years.

Also a huge debt of thanks goes to Marci Cervone, without whose wisdom, generosity of spirit, faith, love, and encouragement I would surely be less than—in life and in literature.

And for holding my virtual hand in our longstanding coffee klatch for the better part of the past decade, Carole Moore, whose no-nonsense attitude, wicked humor, and daily support and friendship has helped nurture me through this project as she always does.

And finally to the loves of my life, Andrew and Ashley Nelson, for their constant encouragement, outrageous opinions, interesting discussions, and their wit, wisdom, intelligence, love, and support. I love you.

About the Author

*J*ennifer Nelson is a successful freelance writer, public speaker, and journalist. Over the past fifteen years, she's written hundreds of articles on health, parenting, relationships, pop culture, pets, and travel for practically every women's magazine on the newsstand.

When she's not writing for women's glossies, she contributes to a variety of publications, including *The Washington Post, The Chicago Tribune, Reader's Digest, Parade, AARP,* and other leading magazines and websites.

Nelson teaches Stiletto Boot Camp, a course on women's magazine writing, through Mediabistro, and speaks at conferences around the country.

She is a bonafide women's glossy magazine junkie.

Selected Titles from Seal Press

For more than thirty years, Seal Press has published groundbreaking books. By women. For women.

Hot & Heavy: Fierce Fat Girls on Life, Love & Fashion, by Virgie Tovar. $16.00, 978-1-58005-438-6. A fun, fresh anthology that celebrates positive body image, feeling comfortable in one's own skin, and being fabulously fine with being fat.

The Purity Myth: How America's Obsession with Virginity Is Hurting Young Women, by Jessica Valenti. $16.95, 978-1-58005-314-3. With her usual balance of intelligence and wit, Valenti presents a powerful argument that girls and women, even in this day and age, are overly valued for their sexuality—and that this needs to stop.

Beautiful You: A Daily Guide to Radical Self-Acceptance, by Rosie Molinary. $16.95, 978-1-58005-331-0. A practical, accessible, day-by-day guide to redefining beauty and building lasting self-esteem from body expert Rosie Molinary.

Reality Bites Back: The Troubling Truth About Guilty Pleasure TV, by Jennifer L. Pozner. $16.95, 978-1-58005-265-8. Deconstructs reality TV's twisted fairytales to demonstrate that they are far from being simple "guilty pleasures," and arms readers with the tools they need to understand and challenge the stereotypes reality TV reinforces.

Body Outlaws: Rewriting the Rules of Beauty and Body Image, edited by Ophira Edut, foreword by Rebecca Walker. $15.95, 978-1-58005-108-8. Filled with honesty and humor, this groundbreaking anthology offers stories by women who have chosen to ignore, subvert, or redefine the dominant beauty standard in order to feel at home in their bodies.

Find Seal Press Online
www.SealPress.com
www.Facebook.com/SealPress
Twitter: @SealPress